brilliant

Microsoft® PowerPoint 2007

POCKET BOOK

S. E. Slack

Harlow, England • London • New York • Boston • San Francisco • Toronto
Sydney • Tokyo • Singapore • Hong Kong • Seoul • Taipei • New Delhi
Cape Town • Madrid • Mexico City • Amsterdam • Munich • Paris • Milan

PEARSON EDUCATION LIMITED

Edinburgh Gate
Harlow CM20 2JE
Tel: +44 (0)1279 623623
Fax: +44 (0)1279 431059
Website: www.pearsoned.co.uk

First published in Great Britain in 2007

ISBN: 978-0-132-05969-5

British Library Cataloguing-in-Publication Data
A catalogue record for this book is available from the British Library

Library of Congress Cataloging-in-Publication Data
A catalog record for this book is available from the Library of Congress

10 9 8 7 6 5 4 3 2 1
11 10 09 08 07

Typeset in Helvetica by 3
Printed and bound by Ashford Colour Press, Gosport

The publisher's policy is to use paper manufactured from sustainable forests.

Brilliant Pocket Books

What you need to know – when you need it!

When you're working on your PC and come up against a problem that you're unsure how to solve, or want to accomplish something in an application that you aren't sure how to do, where do you look? If you are fed up with wading through pages of background information in unwieldy manuals and training guides trying to find the piece of information or advice that you need RIGHT NOW, and if you find that helplines really aren't that helpful, then Brilliant Pocket Books are the answer!

Brilliant Pocket Books have been developed to allow you to find the info that you need easily and without fuss and to guide you through each task using a highly visual step-by-step approach – providing exactly what you need to know, when you need it!

Brilliant Pocket Books are concise, easy-to-access guides to all of the most common, important and useful tasks in all of the applications in the Office 2007 suite. Short, concise lessons make it really easy to learn any particular feature, or master any task or problem that you will come across in day-to-day use of the applications.

When you are faced with any task on your PC, whether major or minor, that you are unsure about, your Brilliant Pocket Book will provide you with the answer – almost before you know what the question is!

Brilliant Pocket Books Series

Series Editor: Joli Ballew

Brilliant Microsoft® Access 2007 Pocket Book	*S.E. Slack*
Brilliant Microsoft® Excel 2007 Pocket Book	*J. Peter Bruzzese*
Brilliant Microsoft® Office 2007 Pocket Book	*Jerri Ledford & Rebecca Freshour*
Brilliant Microsoft® Outlook 2007 Pocket Book	*Meryl K. Evans*
Brilliant Microsoft® PowerPoint 2007 Pocket Book	*S.E. Slack*
Brilliant Microsoft® Windows Vista Pocket Book	*Jerri Ledford & Rebecca Freshour*
Brilliant Windows Microsoft® Word 2007 Pocket Book	*Deanna Reynolds*

Contents

Introduction   x

1   **Using PowerPoint 2007**   1
→ What's New in PowerPoint?   2
→ Starting PowerPoint   4
→ Customising PowerPoint   6
   – Customising the Quick Access Toolbar   6
   – Customising other Options   8
→ Working with PowerPoint File Formats   10
→ Using AutoRecover Setting   12
→ Using Spelling and Grammar Options   13
   – Using Smart Tags   15
→ Exiting PowerPoint   16

2   **Getting Started with PowerPoint**   17
→ Starting a New Presentation   18
   – Using a Template   21
   – Using an Existing Presentation   25
   – Using a Blank Presentation   26
→ Adding Slides to Your Presentation   28
→ Deleting a Slide   30
→ Adding Watermarks to Your Slides   31
→ Preparing Your Presentations   33
   – Document Inspector   34
   – Mark as Final   37
→ Saving and Closing a Presentation   38
   – Saving Your Presentation in Different Ways   38
   – Closing Your Presentation   39

3   **Working with Presentation Views**   41
→ Understanding Presentation Views   42
   – Changing Views   42
   – Normal View   43
   – Slide Sorter View   43

–	Notes Page View	46
–	Slide Show View	46
→	Using the Outline Tab	47
→	Changing the Default View of Your Presentation	48

4 Working with the Master Views **51**
→	Understanding Master Views	52
→	Creating and Using the Slide Master	53
–	Removing Unwanted Slides	55
–	Removing Unwanted Placeholders	56
–	Adding New Placeholders	56
–	Adding Custom Text to a Placeholder	57
–	Adding a Theme	57
–	Modifying the Background	57
–	Setting Page Orientation	58
–	Adding Custom Text to Slide Footers	59
–	Renaming a Slide Master	60
–	Renaming a Slide Layout	60
→	Using the Handout Master	61
–	Opening the Handout Master	61
–	Working with Handout Master Footers and Headers	62
–	Using the Date Feature	63
–	Using the Page Number Feature	64
→	Using the Notes Master	64
–	Changing the Font	65
–	Changing the Font Colour	65
–	Changing the Font Size	66
–	Aligning Text	66

5 Creating a Look for Your Presentation **69**
→	Using Colour Schemes	70
→	Using Themes	73
–	Customising a Theme	74
–	Applying a Theme to a Single Slide	76
→	Applying Design Templates	78
→	Working with Background Styles	80
→	Changing Slide Orientation	83
→	Modifying Page Setup	85

6 Creating Slide Text 87

→ Creating a Text Box 88
→ Working with Fonts 90
 – Adding Bold, Italic and Underlining to Text 90
 – Adding a Shadow to Text 90
 – Editing Text by Using Strikethrough 91
→ Working with Text Size, Alignment and Spacing 92
 – Changing Text Size 92
 – Changing Text Alignment 92
 – Changing Line Spacing 93
 – Changing Character Spacing 94
 – Changing Sentence Case 95
→ Changing Text Direction 96
→ Adding Colour, Outline and Effects to Text 98
→ Using QuickStyles 100
 – The Shapes Gallery 100
 – The Shape Styles Gallery 103
 – The WordArt Gallery 104

7 Working with Graphics 107

→ Understanding how Graphics are Used in a Presentation 108
→ Adding Pictures 108
→ The Adjust Group 109
 – Brightness 109
 – Contrast 110
 – Recolor 111
 – Compress Pictures 111
 – Change Picture 113
 – Reset Picture 113
→ The Picture Styles Group 114
 – The Picture Styles QuickStyle Gallery 114
 – Turning Pictures into Shapes 115
 – Changing a Picture Border 117
→ The Arrange Group 117
 – Placing a Picture in Front of or Behind another Object 118
 – Using the Selection Pane 118
 – Using the Size Group 120
→ Adding Clip Art 120
→ Using SmartArt 122

→ Adding Charts   127
  – Saving a Chart Template   129
  – Formatting Chart Elements   129

8 Adding Columns, Tables and Lists   131

→ Working with Columns   132
→ Working with Tables   133
  – Adding a Table   134
  – Understanding and Applying Table Styles   137
  – Drawing a Table   139
  – Copying a Table from Word or Excel   139
  – Inserting a Table Directly from Excel   140
  – Changing Colours in a Table   140
  – Working with Grid Lines   141
→ Working with Lists   142

9 Adding Animation to Your Presentation   147

→ Working with Sound   148
  – Adding Basic Sound   149
  – Modifying Stop and Start Settings   150
  – Playing a CD During a Presentation   154
  – Package for CD   155
→ Working with Media Clips   157
→ Adding Slide Animation   160
  – Creating a Simple Animation   161
  – Creating a Simple Motion Path   161
  – Creating a Custom Animation Path   163
  – Changing Animation Order   163
→ Animating SmartArt Graphics   164
→ Using Slide Transitions   166

10 Working with PowerPoint Objects   169

→ Selecting an Object   170
→ Using Layered Objects   171
  – Grouping and Ungrouping Objects   172
  – Converting a SmartArt Graphic to Individual Shapes   173
→ Cutting, Copying and Pasting Objects   174
  – Using the Paste Special Command   175
  – Using the Office Clipboard   176

→ Moving, Rotating and Resizing Objects   179

  – Moving an Object   179

  – Rotating an Object   180

  – Resizing an Object   181

  – Working with Grids and Guidelines   186

11 Working with Slide Shows   189

→ Rehearsing the Slide Show   190

  – Rehearsing the Timing of Your Presentation   190

  – Setting Slide Timings Manually   192

  – Adding Narration   193

→ Using Presenter View   194

→ Writing on Slides During a Presentation   197

→ Creating Custom Shows   198

  – Creating a Basic Custom Show   199

  – Creating a Hyperlinked Custom Show   201

  – Running a Custom Show   202

→ Using Photo Albums   203

  – Working with Captions in Your Photo Album   205

  – Publishing Your Photo Album to the Web   206

12 Completing Your Presentation   209

→ Choosing what to Print   210

→ Using Print Preview   210

→ Printing Your Presentation   212

→ Using the Quick Print Option   213

→ Changing Page Setup   215

→ Publishing Your Presentation to a Slide Library   216

  – Publishing Slides to a Slide Library   217

Introduction

Welcome to the *Brilliant Microsoft® Power Point 2007 Pocket Book* – a handy, visual quick reference that will give you a basic grounding in the common features and tasks that you will need to master to use Microsoft® PowerPoint 2007 in any day-to-day situation. Keep it on your desk, in your briefcase or bag – or even in your pocket! – and you will always have the answer to hand for any problem or task that you come across.

Find out what you need to know – when you need it!

You don't have to read this book in any particular order. It is designed so that you can jump in, get the information you need and jump out – just look up the task in the contents list, turn to the right page, read the introduction, follow the step-by-step instructions – and you're done!

How this book works

Each section in this book includes foolproof step-by-step instructions for performing specific tasks, using screenshots to illustrate each step. Additional information is included to help increase your understanding and develop your skills – these are identified by the following icons:

 Jargon buster – New or unfamiliar terms are defined and explained in plain English to help you as you work through a section.

 Timesaver tip – These tips give you ideas that cut corners and confusion. They also give you additional information related to the topic that you are currently learning. Use them to expand your knowledge of a particular feature or concept.

 Important – This identifies areas where new users often run into trouble, and offers practical hints and solutions to these problems.

Brilliant Pocket Books are a handy, accessible resource that you will find yourself turning to time and time again when you are faced with a problem or an unfamiliar task and need an answer at your fingertips – or in your pocket!

1

Using PowerPoint 2007

In this chapter, you will learn about new features and capabilities in PowerPoint 2007, as well as how to start, customise and exit PowerPoint. You'll also discover how to use PowerPoint's new AutoRecover and spelling features.

→ What's New in PowerPoint?

The first thing you'll notice in PowerPoint 2007 is the new interface. There is a tabbed navigational structure that displays functions, tools and commands in the order most people commonly perform tasks. This structure, along with a File button, Quick Access Toolbar and a View toolbar with a Zoom slider, replaces the dropdown menus used in previous versions of PowerPoint.

The tabbed navigational structure is actually called the "Ribbon". It is shown in Figure 1.1.

Inside each Ribbon tab is a command group that holds the commands you need. For example, on the Home tab, there are six command groups: Clipboard, Slides, Font, Paragraph, Drawing and Editing.

Within each command group are various commands. The Editing command group holds the commands Find, Replace and Select, while the Clipboard group holds commands such as Paste, Cut, Copy and Format Painter. So, when you are trying to find the commands to cut and paste, you would select the Home tab and then use the Cut and Paste commands within it.

PowerPoint 2007 commands number more than 1000, so there will be plenty that you'll discover on your own since this book can't cover them all. As you work with the commands, there are two things to remember. First, the commands are contextual. This means that some commands are not available until a previous command or option is selected – commands are

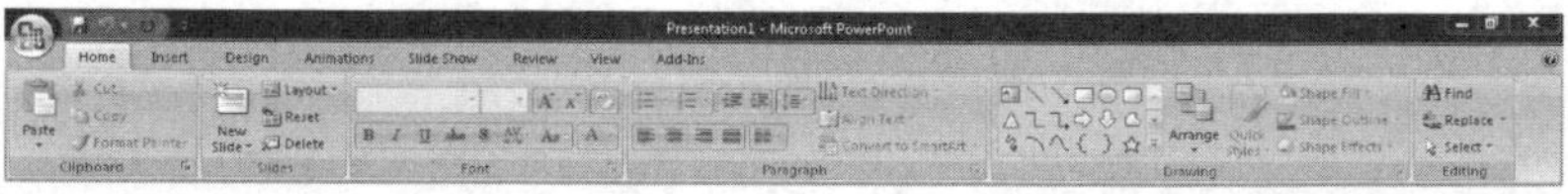

Figure 1.1
PowerPoint 2007 uses the Ribbon to help you navigate commands and tools quickly and easily.

provided to you based on the context of the work you are performing within PowerPoint.

1

Timesaver tip

Looking for a command? Check PowerPoint 2007 Help and Support. Type "commands" in the search box and then select **Interactive: PowerPoint 2003 to PowerPoint 2007 Command Reference Guide**. Click **Start the Guide** and the interactive tutorial will instantly show you where commands are located in PowerPoint 2007 by letting you select familiar commands from PowerPoint 2003.

Second, there are multiple ways to perform most commands. For example, if you want to print a document, you can do it through the Office button, the Quick Access Toolbar and the Print Preview tab. This multiple approach to commands makes it easy to find the command you need when you need it. As you become more familiar with PowerPoint 2007, you'll be able to determine which command works best for you in a given situation.

Other new features and tools include the following:

- Predefined themes
- QuickStyles
- Custom slide layouts
- SmartArt graphics
- Improved table formats
- Enhanced effects
- New text options
- Improved spellchecker features
- Presenter View
- New file formats
- Increased security features.

→ Starting PowerPoint

You can start PowerPoint from the Start button in Windows Vista by following these steps:

1 Click the **Start** button.

2 Click **All Programs**.

3 Click the **Microsoft Office** folder.

4 Click **Microsoft Office PowerPoint 2007**, as shown in Figure 1.2.

PowerPoint will open to a blank presentation. The next time you click the Start button, PowerPoint 2007 should be shown in the

Figure 1.2
Open PowerPoint through the Windows Vista Start menu.

lower left pane of the Start menu. It will continue to show there until you have opened more programs and PowerPoint drops off the list automatically.

If you plan to use PowerPoint often, you should make it a permanent part of the Start menu. Follow these steps to pin PowerPoint permanently to the Start menu:

1 Click the **Start** button.

2 Locate PowerPoint 2007. If it is not shown in the Start menu, you will need to click the **Microsoft Office** folder to find it.

3 Right-click **PowerPoint 2007**.

4 Click **Pin to Start Menu**, as shown in Figure 1.3.

The next time you want to open PowerPoint, just click the **Start** button and click **Microsoft Office PowerPoint 2007** in the top left pane. If you ever want to remove it from that permanent position, follow these steps:

1 Right-click **Microsoft Office PowerPoint 2007**.

2 Click **Unpin from Start Menu**.

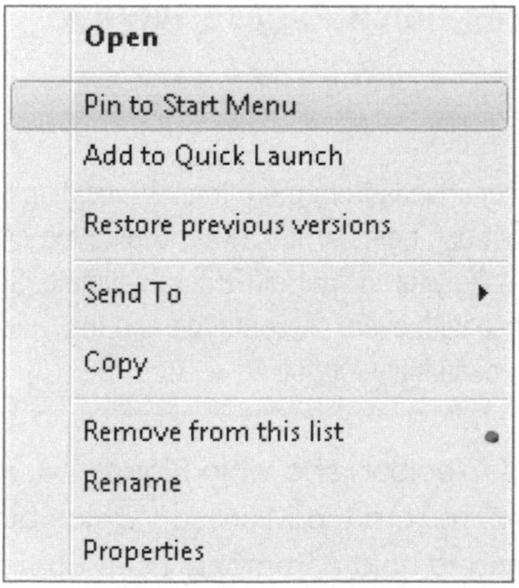

Open

Pin to Start Menu

Add to Quick Launch

Restore previous versions

Send To ▶

Copy

Remove from this list ●

Rename

Properties

Figure 1.3
You can pin or unpin items to the Start Menu

→ Customising PowerPoint

A new PowerPoint presentation will open automatically with seven
tabs: Home, Insert, Design, Animations, Slide Show, Review and
View. The initial tab that will open for you in a new presentation is
the Home tab. Other tabs will appear as appropriate. For
example, in Figure 1.1, the Add-Ins tab is shown because some
additional items were added into the author's version.

You can customize PowerPoint 2007 in two ways: through the
File menu of the Microsoft Office button and through the
Quick Access Toolbar.

Customising the Quick Access Toolbar

The Quick Access Toolbar, shown in Figure 1.4, is located just
above the Ribbon, next to the Microsoft Office button. This
toolbar is designed to hold commonly used commands for easy
access. Default commands of Save As, Undo and Repeat are
displayed in every document, but you can add more commands

Figure 1.4
The Quick Access Toolbar is handy for accessing commonly used commands.

to it whenever you want. When you need one of the commands, simply click the command from the Quick Access Toolbar instead of using tabs or other lengthier options to find a command.

For example, if you often use the Italics command to italicise fonts, you can simply add that command to the Quick Access Toolbar so it's always visible and available to you. To add a command to the Quick Access Toolbar, follow these steps:

1 Locate the command in PowerPoint 2007.

2 Right-click the command.

3 Click **Add to Quick Access Toolbar**, as shown in Figure 1.5.

Timesaver tip

Look closely at the Quick Access Toolbar. Just to its right is a dropdown arrow. Click the arrow and you'll see a menu of popular options that you might want to add to your toolbar. If you see an option you like, click it and it will automatically be added to the toolbar.

> Add to Quick Access Toolbar
>
> Customize Quick Access Toolbar...
>
> Show Quick Access Toolbar Below the Ribbon
>
> Minimize the Ribbon

Figure 1.5
A simple click adds items to the Quick Access Toolbar

Customising other Options

If you want to customise the overall user interface, such as the look and feel of PowerPoint or other individual options, use the PowerPoint Options dialogue box. There are eight customisation options available: Popular, Proofing, Save, Advanced, Customize, Add-Ins, Trust Center and Resources, as Figure 1.6 shows.

Popular

To modify the look and feel of PowerPoint 2007, you will want to work with this option. You can vary the colour scheme, select languages and enable or disable functions such as Mini Toolbars, ScreenTips, Live Previews, Developer tabs and ClearType. You can also change your user name and initials with this option.

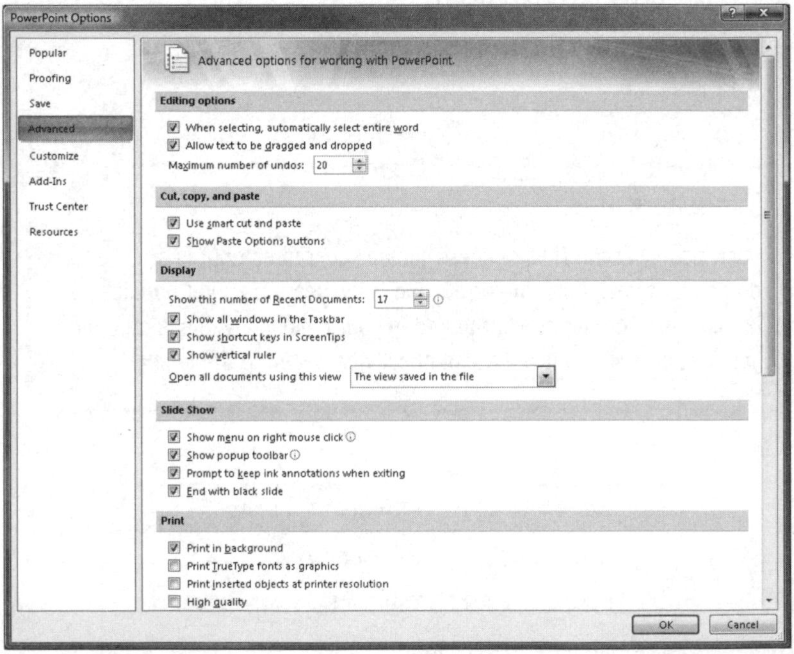

Figure 1.6
PowerPoint Options offers a multitude of ways to customise PowerPoint 2007 to your needs.

Proofing

This option lets you choose how PowerPoint formats or corrects text. Spelling, dictionary and auto-correction settings are shown here. Note that there are two different areas for spelling corrections: spelling correction options can be changed in all Office programs as well as in PowerPoint.

Save

With this option, you can customise how – and how often – documents are saved. Preferences such as file format and AutoRecover settings, offline editing options and embedded font information for file-sharing purposes are all provided here.

Advanced

Editing, display and print options are available with this option. In addition, you can customise Web options by using more than 50 possibilities to tailor your PowerPoint presentation for the Web.

Customize

This is the area previously mentioned under Customize The Quick Access Toolbar.

Add-Ins

This customisation option lets you manage PowerPoint or COM Add-Ins, SmartTags and disabled Items by active or inactive status. It also shows you template files for currently open documents as well as add-ins that have been disabled.

Trust Center

A new feature with PowerPoint 2007, the Trust Center allows you to choose privacy and security options such as macro settings, Active-X controls and trusted publishers. These preset options have been determined by Microsoft to be the most secure settings for users, so make any changes with extreme caution.

Resources

Use this option to contact Microsoft, acquire updates, activate Office programs and carry out diagnostic tests. You can also sign up for free online services.

To open the PowerPoint Options dialogue box, follow these steps:

1 Click the **Microsoft Office** button.

2 Click **PowerPoint Options**.

3 Select the option you want to work with:

■ Click the option you want in the left pane, and follow the instructions provided or choose from the options provided in the right pane. Most of the time, an option can be customised by placing or removing a checkmark in a box.

4 After you have made your selections in a given option, click **OK**.

Jargon buster

XML An abbreviation for Extensible Markup Language, a technology that lets data be structured, validated, repurposed and reorganised with each new use. It's a pretty widely accepted standard in the computer industry, but it is still fairly new to the general public. Information stored in this format allows any computer system to read it.

→ Working with PowerPoint File Formats

When you work with PowerPoint 2007, you'll notice that there is a new default file format called *.pptx*. The previous default file format in earlier versions of PowerPoint was *.ppt*. This new file format is used because PowerPoint 2007 uses Office Extensible Markup Language (XML) to help with data compression, file recovery and integration with other kinds of content.

With PowerPoint, files can become quite large, especially if a lot of graphics are used. The new XML file format substantially reduces files sizes, which in turn can improve storage and bandwidth capabilities on your computer. It also segments data on your hard drive so that even if part of your presentation becomes corrupted, other parts of the presentation can be recovered. This format also makes it easier for you to access data from Word or Excel when using PowerPoint 2007.

In Table 1.1, you can see all the file extensions now associated with PowerPoint 2007.

Table 1.1 **File Types and Correlating Extensions for PowerPoint 2007**

Standard File Types	Related File Extension
PowerPoint 97–2003 presentation	.ppt
PowerPoint 97–2003 template	.pot
PowerPoint 97–2003 show	.pps
PowerPoint 97–2003 add-in	.ppa
File Types Available with Add-Ins	**File Extension**
XML Paper Specification (XPS)	.xps
Portable Document Format (PDF)	.pdf
XML File Types	**File Extension**
PowerPoint 2007 presentation	.pptx
PowerPoint XML presentation	.xml
Macro-enabled presentation	.pptm
Template	.potx
Macro-enabled template	.potm
Macro-enabled add-in	.ppam
Show	.ppsx
Autonomous slide file	.sldx
Macro-enabled slide	.sldm
Office theme	.thmx

Important

You may experience difficulties working with people who do not have PowerPoint 97 or a later version. That's because in PowerPoint 2007, you can't save a file as PowerPoint 95 or earlier. Instead, save it as a PDF or XPS file (see Chapter 2 for more details).

→ Using AutoRecover Setting

In PowerPoint, it's not uncommon to have multiple slides open at the same time. People often cut or copy and paste information from one presentation to another. Plus, you can have other programs open at the same time. All those open programs and activities can occasionally cause your computer to crash. The last thing you need if that happens is to lose all your work.

Through the AutoRecover option, Microsoft has improved PowerPoint's ability to save and recover files when this type of catastrophe occurs. By specifying a few settings, you can ensure that your presentation is automatically saved – and therefore recoverable – every few minutes.

To establish AutoRecover settings, follow these steps:

1 Click the **Microsoft Office** button.

2 Click **PowerPoint Options**.

3 Select **Save**.

4 Place a checkmark in the box **Save AutoRecover Information every X Minutes**, as shown in Figure 1. 7.

5 Using the up and down arrows on the same line as the checkmark, select the number of minutes for the AutoRecover information to occur.

6 Click **OK**.

Important

You should always save a presentation manually in addition to using AutoRecover settings.

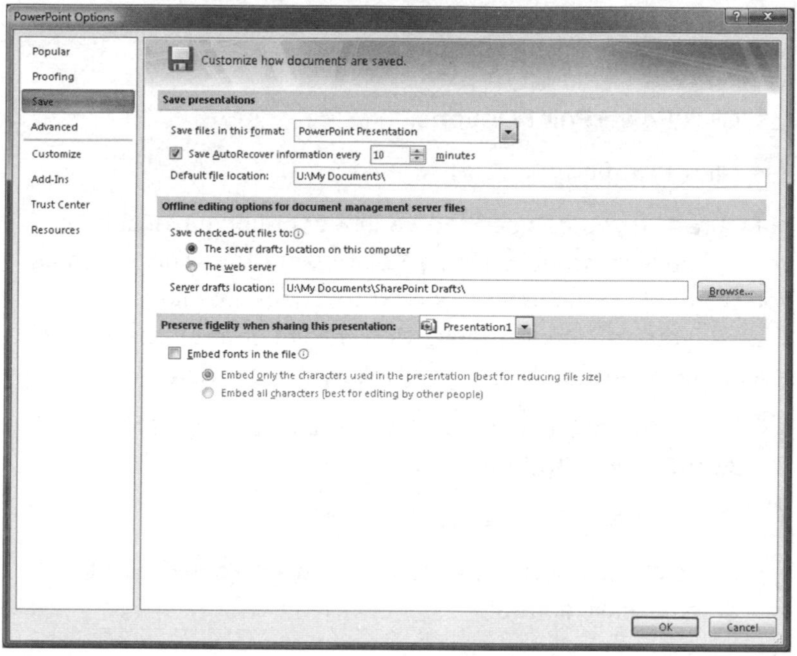

Figure 1.7
AutoRecover options can be set easily to help you recover information quickly during a system crash.

→ Using Spelling and Grammar Options

There have been a few changes to the way spellchecker options work. For example, you can now set many spellchecker options in a "global" manner – set them in one program such as PowerPoint, and they will apply across the board to all other Office programs. Other changes include:

- A post-reform French dictionary is included in PowerPoint 2007.

- An exclusion dictionary lets you flag words you want to avoid using.

- Some contextual spelling errors, such as "their" instead of "there", can be flagged for you. (Note: this option is available only for English, German and Spanish.)

To set proofing options, follow these steps:

1 Click the **Microsoft Office** button.

2 Click **PowerPoint Options**.

3 Click **Proofing**.

In Figure 1.8, you can see the variety of options available to you. If you want to have PowerPoint identify spelling errors as you work, place a checkmark next to Check Spelling as You Type. If you also want to have PowerPoint correct spelling or grammatical errors as you type, follow these steps:

1 In the Proofing section of PowerPoint Options, click **AutoCorrect Options**.

2 Click the **AutoFormat as You Type** tab.

3 Place checkmarks in the items you want PowerPoint to automatically correct.

4 Click the **AutoCorrect** tab.

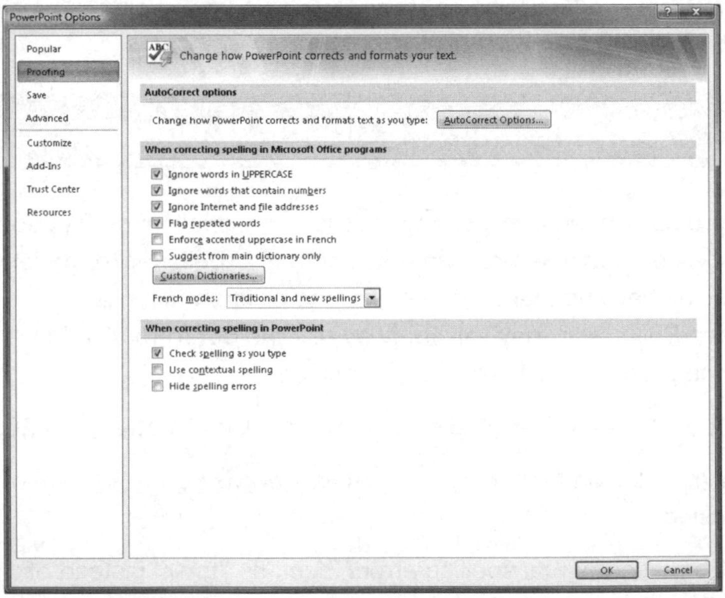

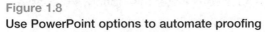

Figure 1.8
Use PowerPoint options to automate proofing

5 Place checkmarks in the items you want PowerPoint to automatically correct. Note: click **Exceptions** if you want to make any exceptions.

6 Click **OK**.

Using Smart Tags

Smart Tags can be used in PowerPoint 2007. These tags recognise types of data – names, dates, telephone numbers, etc. – and let you perform instant actions. For example, if you place a name in PowerPoint, it will be recognised as a "person name" and a Smart Tag attached to it will let you instantly perform actions such as Open Contact and Schedule a Meeting.

You can use Smart Tags in PowerPoint 2007 by following these steps:

1 Click the **Microsoft Office** button.

2 Click **PowerPoint Options**.

3 Click **Proofing**.

4 Click **AutoCorrect Options**.

5 Click the **Smart Tags** tab, as shown in Figure 1.9.

6 Place a checkmark in Label Text with Smart Tags.

7 Choose any or all of the Recognizers (Measurement Converter, Date, Financial Symbol, Person Name) by placing a checkmark in the corresponding box, as Figure 1.9 shows.

8 Click **OK**.

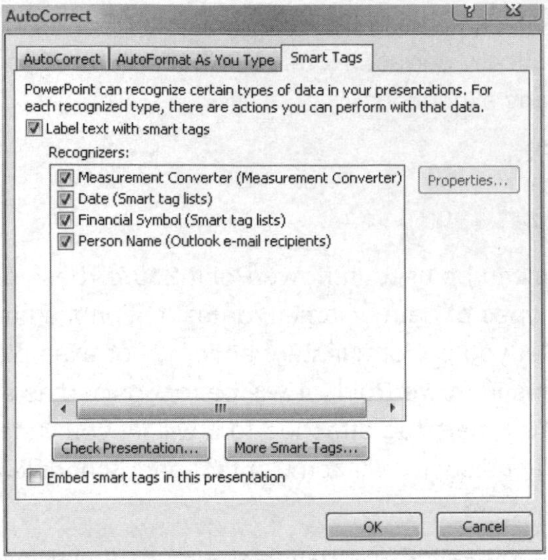

Figure 1.9
Smart tags are easy to add to PowerPoint

→ Exiting PowerPoint

When you want to exit PowerPoint, be sure you have saved the presentation. Then, follow these steps:

1 Click the **Microsoft Office** button.

2 Click **Exit PowerPoint**.

Timesaver tip

You can quickly exit a presentation by clicking the **Microsoft Office** button and then clicking **Close**. However, this option closes only the presentation – it does not close PowerPoint itself.

2

Getting Started with PowerPoint

In this chapter, you will learn how to start a new presentation, work with templates, use the PowerPoint workspace and work with placeholders, open existing presentations and save and close a presentation. You'll also learn about watermarks, how to use the Document Inspector and how to mark your presentation as final.

→ Starting a New Presentation

Starting a new presentation in PowerPoint is a simple process. Follow these steps once you have opened PowerPoint:

1 Click the **Microsoft Office** button.

2 Click **New**. The New Presentation window will appear, as in Figure 2.1.

3 Click **Blank Presentation**.

4 Click **Create**.

A new presentation will appear in Normal View, as shown in Figure 2.2. It's a good idea to familiarise yourself with the PowerPoint workspace, as its four key areas will be referred to repeatedly throughout this book.

Jargon buster

Thumbnail As a miniature version of the full-sized slides in a presentation, thumbnails are helpful because they let you locate slides quickly in a presentation.

The four areas of the PowerPoint workspace are:

- **Slide pane.** This is where you can directly access and work on individual slides within a presentation.

- **Placeholders.** These are used to insert text, pictures, charts, animations and other objects.

- **Slides tab.** In this area, thumbnails of each slide are shown. You can add or delete slides in this area or click and drag thumbnails to rearrange slides.

- **Notes pane.** This is where you can enter notes about a particular slide. Notes do not appear when a presentation is

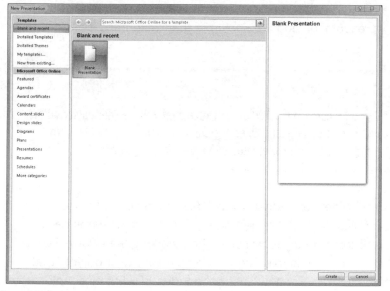

Figure 2.1
PowerPoint New Presentation window

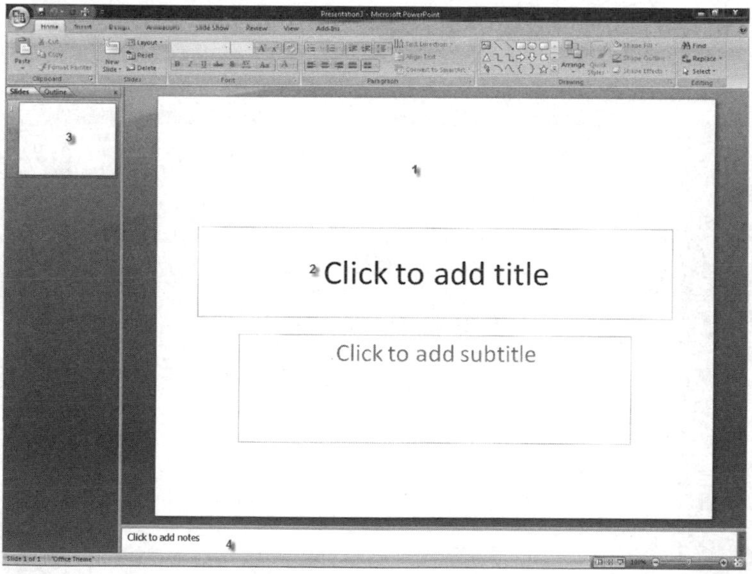

Figure 2.2
Every presentation has four key areas that make up the PowerPoint
workspace.

being run, but they can appear in printed versions of the presentation and are shown in the Presenter View.

Placeholders are added to a slide in many different ways. Graphics, text, charts and other objects are all forms of placeholder that you will use when working with PowerPoint. Later chapters in this book address a variety of objects that use placeholders. For now, just get an idea of what placeholders are and how they generally work.

When you work with a placeholder, just click the edge of it and, when the cursor turns to a double arrow, use the sizing handles, as shown in Figure 2.3, to resize it.

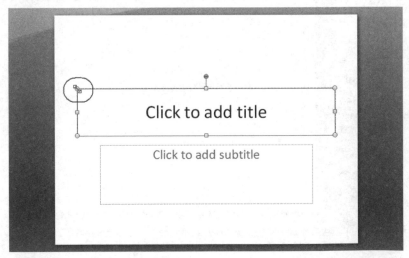

Figure 2.3
Placeholders can be resized easily.

If you need to move a placeholder, click the placeholder and hover the cursor over the placeholder's border. When the cursor turns to a four-sided arrow, as shown in Figure 2.4, click again and drag the placeholder to the new location on the slide.

2

Jargon buster

Template A template is a file that captures customisations made with slide masters, layouts and themes. When you use a template in a business environment, it helps to provide consistency in the look and feel of your department's presentations.

Using a Template

Sometimes, you may want to use a template. Templates are terrific because they have already formatted the presentation for you; you simply fill in the blanks with your content. Depending upon the template you use, you might need to modify certain aspects such as background or colour themes, font or heading styles, slide masters, and placeholder sizes and locations, as shown in Figure 2.4.

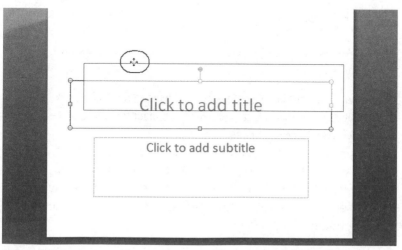

Figure 2.4
Placeholders can be moved quickly using a click-and-drag process.

You can create your own template or use an existing template.

To create a template, follow these steps:

1 Open a slide master. (You can learn how to use slide masters in Chapter 4.)

2 Create the layout for the slide.

3 Click the **Microsoft Office** button.

4 Click **Save As**.

5 Type in a name for the template in the File Name box, or accept the name provided.

6 Click **PowerPoint Templates (*.potx)** in the Save as type list, as shown in Figure 2.5.

7 Select the location where you want the template to be saved to.

8 Click **Save**.

Timesaver tip

You can make your templates easy to find by saving them to the Templates folder. This is located on your computer at *C:\Program Files\Microsoft Office\Templates*.

Instead of creating your own templates, you can also use existing templates that are built in to PowerPoint or are available from other places, such as another presentation or downloaded from Microsoft.

To use an existing template, open PowerPoint and then follow these steps:

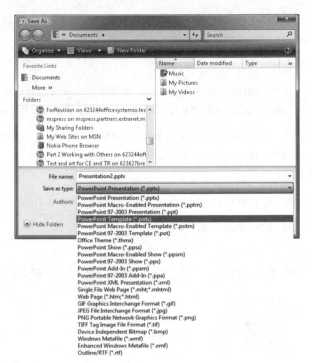

Figure 2.5
You can save presentations as templates

1 Click the **Microsoft Office** button.

2 Click **New**.

3 Make your selection in the Templates pane on the left side of
the New Presentation dialogue box, as shown in Figure 2.6.
Your options are:

  ■ **Blank and recent** – shows you the currently available
  templates in the centre pane.

  ■ **Installed Templates** – shows you templates already
  included with PowerPoint 2007.

  ■ **Installed Themes** – shows you templates with Office
  2007 themes already included in PowerPoint 2007.

  ■ **My templates** – shows you all the templates you have
  created by opening a New Presentation dialogue box.

- **New from existing** – allows you to search your computer for the template.

4 Click **Create**.

At the top of the centre pane is a search box that you can use to search Microsoft Office Online for templates, as shown in Figure 2.7.

These online templates are very simple to download and use. Follow these steps to find and download a template from Microsoft Office Online:

1 Type in the search term you want in the search box.

2 Click the right-hand arrow.

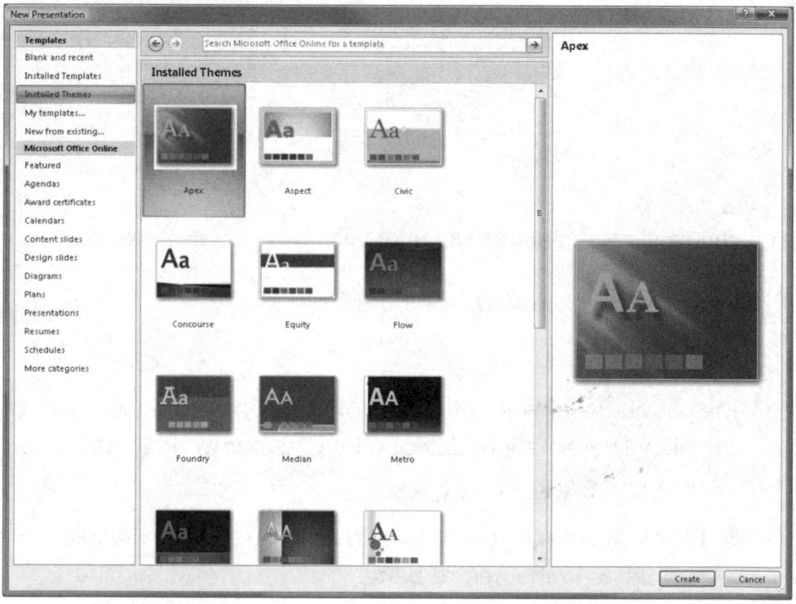

Figure 2.6
You can select from a variety of template options in PowerPoint 2007.

Figure 2.7
Searching for templates is fast and easy

3 Review the search results and select the presentation template you prefer, as shown in Figure 2.8.

4 Click **Download**.

Important

You may see a Microsoft Office Genuine Advantage dialogue box appear, as in Figure 2.9. Click **Continue**. If another dialogue box appears saying that you may have counterfeit software, you will need to resolve the issue before you can download a template.

Using an Existing Presentation

It's not uncommon to start with an existing presentation and then either update it or create a new presentation using elements from the existing one. Probably the most important thing to remember when using an existing publication is to save it before you begin making changes. This ensures that you always have the original presentation available.

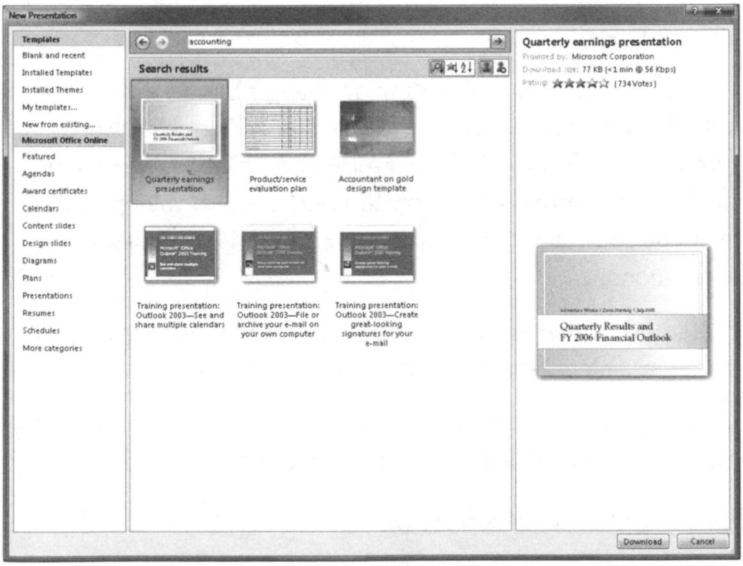

Figure 2.8
Select the template you like from the search results.

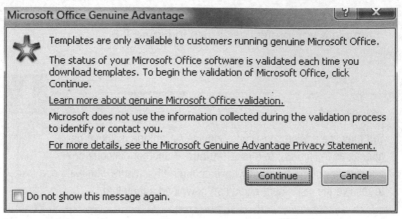

Figure 2.9
You need to complete a simple validation process to download templates

To use an existing presentation, follow these steps:

1 Click the **Microsoft Office** button.

2 Click **Open**.

3 Locate and select the presentation you want to use.

4 Click **Open**.

In the Open dialogue box, you might have noticed a button in the lower left-hand corner above the Open and Cancel buttons. In Figure 2.10, the button is called All PowerPoint Presentations. Click the down arrow on the button and a menu will appear that allows you to broaden or narrow your search for existing presentations.

For example, if you know the presentation you're searching for is a template, select **PowerPoint Templates** to see only templates.

Once the existing presentation is open, you can work with it the same way you would work with any other presentation.

Using a Blank Presentation

Rather than reusing an existing presentation or a template, you might want to start from scratch with your presentation. In that

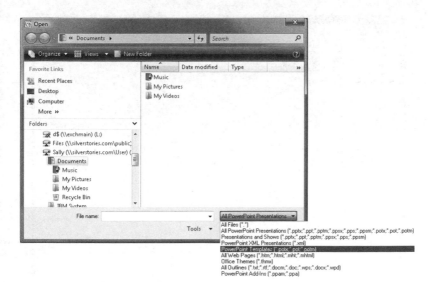

Figure 2.10
You can narrow or broaden a search for an existing presentation using a dropdown menu in the Open dialogue box.

case, you will be creating all aspects of the presentation from scratch, such as backgrounds, themes, headlines and graphics. Some of the items you might need for a blank presentation will be explained here; others will be explained elsewhere in this book. Be sure to read the chapters in the book that show you how to do those things before you create a blank presentation.

To create a blank presentation, follow these steps:

1 Click the **Microsoft Office** button.

2 Click **New**.

3 Click **Blank and recent** in the New Presentation Templates pane, as shown in Figure 2.11.

4 Click **Blank Presentation** in the centre pane.

5 Click **Create**.

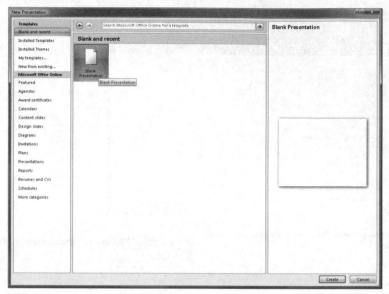

Figure 2.11
Open a blank presentation in the New Presentation window

→ Adding Slides to Your Presentation

To add a new slide, follow these steps:

1 In an open presentation, go to the **Home** tab.

2 Click the slide icon in New Slide in the Slides group, as shown in Figure 2.12.

Figure 2.12
The New Slide command

A Title and Content slide with title and text sections will automatically be placed into your presentation.

Timesaver tip

Just want to duplicate a slide and change a few things on it? Select the slide you want to duplicate in the Slides tab, and then click the down arrow in the New Slide command. Click **Duplicate Selected Slides** and the duplicate slide will be added automatically for you.

If you prefer to add a different type of slide, follow these steps:

1 Go to the **Home** tab.

2 Click the down arrow in the New Slide command, as shown in Figure 2.13.

3 Choose a slide format from the Office Theme gallery, as in Figure 2.14.

4 Click your selection to add it to your presentation.

Timesaver tip

If you want to change the format of your slide quickly, go to the **Home** tab and click **Layout** in the Slides group. Click the new layout you want and PowerPoint will automatically change the slide you are working in. Your content will stay intact on the page, but its location may change.

Figure 2.13
The arrow opens a slide format selection

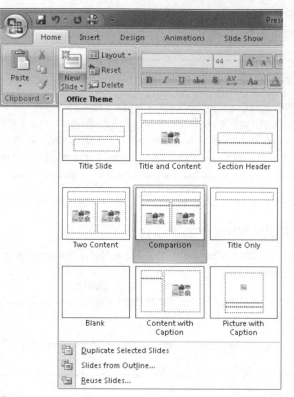

Figure 2.14
Slide Theme gallery

→ Deleting a Slide

When you want to delete a slide, the easiest way to do it is to follow these steps:

1 In the **Slide** tab, click the slide that you want removed.

2 Click **Delete** on your keyboard.

Important

Before you delete a slide, be sure you don't need any of the content! You can't get the content back once a slide has been deleted.

→ Adding Watermarks to Your Slides

Now that you know how to add slides to a presentation, you might want to add a watermark. Watermarks are a great way to identify your slides. Many people use watermarks to identify a presentation or a particular slide as a draft; this is particularly helpful in business situations where there is a possibility that a presentation could get passed around before it is complete.

Jargon buster

Watermark A special, almost transparent but still visible message embedded into a presentation that clearly identifies something for the reader.

Watermarks can be In the form of words or background pictures in PowerPoint 2007. For example, to help readers understand they are not reading a final copy, a "DRAFT" watermark can be shown on a particular slide or even throughout an entire presentation.

Follow these steps to add a text watermark to a presentation:

1 Click the slide where you want the watermark added.

- You can add the watermark to all slides in a blank presentation by clicking **Slide Master** in the Presentation Views group of the View tab. Use the slide master to add the watermark.

2 Go to the **Insert** tab and click **Text Box** in the Text group. Note: you can also select WordArt for this process.

3 Click the slide and draw the text box to the size you need.

4 Enter the text you want.

5 Select a light colour (variations of grey work very well for this) and a font size for the text.

6 When you are satisfied with the appearance of the text, go to the **Format** tab under Drawing Tools. Click **Send to Back** in the Arrange group.

Follow these steps to add a picture as a watermark to a presentation:

1 Click the slide where you want the watermark added.

2 Go to the **Insert** tab and click **Picture** in the Illustrations group. Note: if you prefer to use clip art, select **Clip Art** instead and locate the art you need.

3 Locate the picture you want to use. Click **Insert**.

4 Place the picture where you want it to appear on the slide.

5 With the picture selected, go to the **Format** tab under Picture Tools. In the Adjust group, click **Recolor**.

6 Make a selection under Light Variations by clicking the option you prefer, as in Figure 2.15.

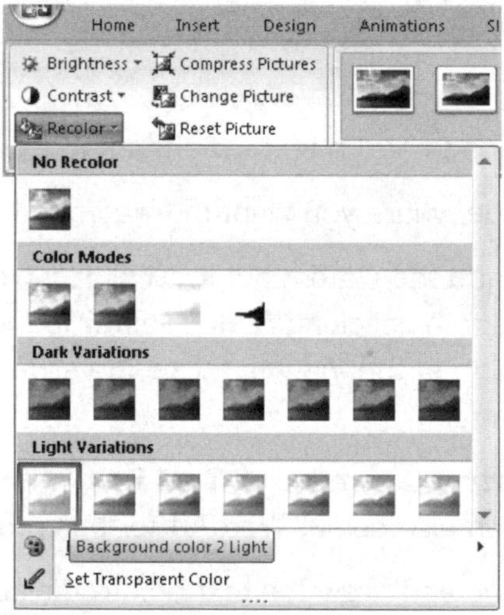

Figure 2.15
Recolor gallery

7 In the Adjust group, click **Brightness**. Click the brightness percentage you prefer.

8 When you are satisfied with the appearance of the text, go to the **Format** tab under Drawing Tools. Click **Send to Back** in the Arrange group.

2

→ Preparing Your Presentations

When you click the **Microsoft Office** button, you might have noticed the Prepare command. This command allows you to prepare your presentation for distribution in different ways. You can choose from the following commands within Prepare (Figure 2.16):

- **Properties** – view or edit the properties (title, author, etc.) in your presentation with this option.

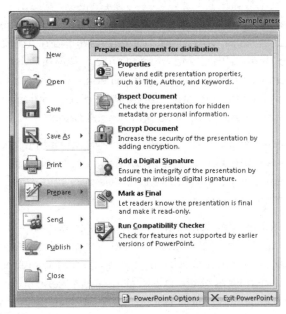

Figure 2.16
PowerPoint offers numerous options to prepare your presentation for distribution

- **Inspect Document** – check your presentation for hidden information that you might not want others to see.

- **Encrypt Document** – add encryption to your presentation to increase security.

- **Add a Digital Signature** – add an invisible digital signature to the presentation.

- **Mark as Final** – show readers that a presentation is final and mark it Read Only.

- **Run Compatibility Checker** – determine whether your presentation has features in it that earlier versions of PowerPoint can't support.

All of these options to prepare your document are important, but two in particular are worth noting: Document Inspector and Mark as Final.

Document Inspector

Sometimes, your presentation might have personal or sensitive information in it that you might not realise is there. To help you locate and remove this kind of information, PowerPoint 2007 has a Document Inspector feature that will search your presentation for different pieces of information and help you remove items you don't want others to see, including the following:

- **Comments and annotations** – this kind of data allows others to see the names of people who made edits to your documents, any comments from reviewers and other changes made to the document.

- **Document properties and personal information** – this is information such as the name of the person who saved the document most recently, when the document was created, and personal identifiers such as e-mail headers, send-for-review information, routing slips, printer paths and file path information.

- **Custom XML data** – this is identifying coding data that PowerPoint generates.

- **Invisible on-slide content** – this is information such as hidden text. Objects formatted as invisible for placeholder or other reasons can sometimes be discovered by others.

- **Off-slide content** – this refers to items that were pulled into the off-slide area, such as text boxes, clip art, tables and graphics.

- **Presentation notes** – the Notes pane of a presentation doesn't appear on the screen. However, notes do appear when a presentation is opened in other modes. The Document Inspector helps you find notes that you may not want others to see.

When the Document Inspector discovers something, it's up to you whether or not to remove the information. To use the Document Inspector, follow these steps:

1 Click the **Microsoft Office** button.

2 Point to **Prepare**.

3 Click **Inspect Document**, as in Figure 2.17.

4 In the Document Inspector dialogue box, select the corresponding checkboxes for the information you want the Document Inspector to search for, as shown in Figure 2.18.

5 Click **Inspect**.

6 When the search is complete, a dialogue box will appear with the inspection results. To remove all the items, click the **Remove All** button, shown in Figure 2.19.

7 Click **Close**. Note: you can also click **Reinspect** to confirm the items have been removed.

Timesaver tip

Don't want to remove all the items the Document Inspector finds? No problem: just go into the document and remove individual items.

Figure 2.17
Inspect Document command

	Document Inspector
	To check the document for the selected content, click Inspect.
☑	**Comments and Annotations**
	Inspects the document for comments and ink annotations.
☑	**Document Properties and Personal Information**
	Inspects for hidden metadata or personal information saved with the document.
☑	**Custom XML Data**
	Inspects for custom XML data stored with this document.
☑	**Invisible On-Slide Content**
	Inspects the presentation for objects that are not visible because they have been formatted as invisible. This does not include objects that are covered by other objects.
☐	**Off-Slide Content**
	Inspects the presentation for objects that are not visible because they are outside the slide area. This does not include objects with animation effects.
☑	**Presentation Notes**
	Inspects the presentation for information in the presenter's notes.

Inspect   Close

Figure 2.18
Document Inspector choices

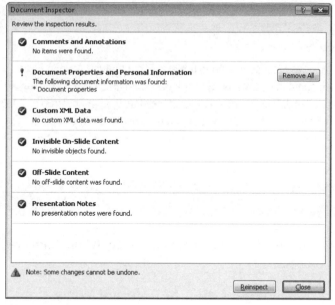

Figure 2.19
Document Inspector results

Mark as Final

The Mark as Final command is useful when you want to prevent readers from accidentally making changes to your presentation. When you use Mark as Final, editing commands, proofing remarks and typing abilities are completely disabled for anyone viewing the document. Essentially, the presentation is opened by others in a read-only format when you apply the Mark as Final command.

To mark a presentation as final, follow these steps:

1 Click the **Microsoft Office** button.

2 Point to **Prepare**.

3 Click **Mark as Final**.

4 Click **OK**.

Important

The Mark as Final command is not a security feature. Anyone can turn editing commands back on within a presentation simply by turning off Mark as Final. Plus, a presentation marked as final in PowerPoint 2007 will not be read-only if opened in earlier versions of PowerPoint.

→ Saving and Closing a Presentation

Whether you need to save or close a presentation, both are very simple processes.

Saving Your Presentation in Different Ways

To save a presentation, you first need to decide upon the file format you want to use. (File formats are reviewed in Chapter 1.) To save a presentation in PowerPoint 2007 format (*.pptx), follow these steps:

1 Click the **Microsoft Office** button.

2 Point to **Save As**.

3 Click **PowerPoint Presentation**.

4 Type in the file name for the presentation and select the location where you want the file to be saved.

5 Verify that the Save As Type is *PowerPoint Presentation (*.pptx)*.

6 Click **Save**.

To save a presentation in an earlier format of PowerPoint, follow these steps:

1 Click the **Microsoft Office** button.

2 Point to **Save As**.

3 Click **PowerPoint 97 – 2003 Presentation**.

4 Type in the file name for the presentation and select the location where you want the file to be saved.

5 Verify that the Save As Type is *PowerPoint 97–2003 Presentation (*.ppt)*.

6 Click **Save**.

You can also save your presentation so that it always opens in slide show mode. It's a good idea to save it as a *.pptx or *.ppt file first, and then make a separate copy that opens only in slide show mode. Follow these steps to save a presentation so that it always opens in slide show mode:

1 Click the **Microsoft Office** button.

2 Point to **Save As**.

3 Click **PowerPoint Show**.

4 Type in the file name for the presentation and select the location where you want the file to be saved.

5 Verify that the Save As Type is *PowerPoint Show (*.ppsx)*.

6 Click **Save**.

Closing Your Presentation

Before you close a presentation, be sure you have saved it. Then, to close a presentation while keeping PowerPoint open, follow these steps:

1 Click the **Microsoft Office** button.

2 Click **Close**.

3

Working with Presentation Views

PowerPoint allows you to work on presentations in four different views. In this chapter, you will learn what those views are and how to use the following aspects of PowerPoint: Outline tab, Slide Sorter, Notes pane and Slide Show.

→ Understanding Presentation Views

When you work on a presentation in PowerPoint, you are working in what's known as a "view". There are four views to work with:

- **Normal** – write content, rearrange slides, work on the current slide and make notes.

- **Slide Sorter** – see all your slides at once using a thumbnail format and a scroll bar.

- **Notes Page** – use a full-page format when creating notes.

- **Slide Show** – see your presentation the same way your audience will, so you can test timing and other aspects before presenting.

Important

There are other views in PowerPoint, too. The Master View is explained in Chapter 4 and the Presenter View is discussed in Chapter 11.

Changing Views

You can easily change views in a presentation by following these steps:

1 In an open presentation, click the **View** tab.

2 Make a new view selection in the Presentation Views group, as shown in Figure 3.1.

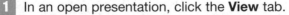

Figure 3.1
You can choose from four different views when working on a presentation.

Normal View

Most people work on presentations in the Normal view, as shown in Figure 3.2. That's because this view allows you to write, edit and design your presentation easily by using the PowerPoint workspace. This is the default view for PowerPoint, so you will see it every time you open a presentation, unless you decide to change the default to a different view (see "Changing the Default View of Your Presentation" later in this chapter).

Because Normal view lets you work on multiple areas at once, it's a good idea to resize each area to a size that works effectively for you. To resize the Slides/Outline pane, click its right border and narrow or widen it as desired. To resize the Notes pane, click its top border to narrow or widen it.

Slide Sorter View

The Slide Sorter view is particularly helpful when you need to rearrange slides. Instead of trying to use the Slide tab to make

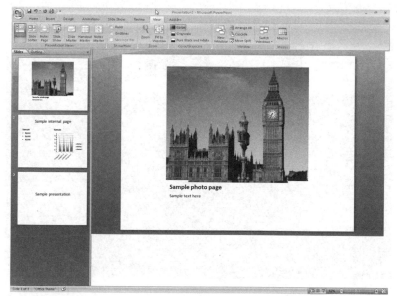

Figure 3.2
Most people work in Normal view in PowerPoint.

changes in the slide order, you can see all of your slides in a larger layout like the one shown in Figure 3.3.

Timesaver tip

You can also move slides in the Slides tab using the drag-and-drop method used in Slide Sorter view.

Adjusting the size of slides

You can adjust the size of the slides in Slide Sorter view to a certain degree by following these steps:

1 In Slide Sorter view, click **Zoom** in the Zoom group.

2 Select the Zoom to percentage you prefer, as shown in Figure 3.4.

3 Click **OK**.

Figure 3.3
Slide Sorter view shows you all your slides in a thumbnail or larger format so you can easily adjust the flow of your presentation.

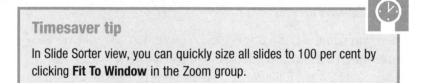

Figure 3.4
The Zoom feature

Changing slide locations

To change the location of a slide in your layout, follow these steps:

1 In Slide Sorter view, click the slide you want to move.

2 Drag the slide to the new location in the layout. A red vertical line will appear between slides to let you know where a slide can be dropped, as Figure 3.5 shows.

3 Let go of the slide.

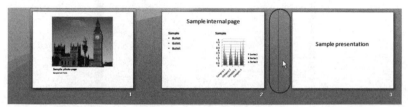

Figure 3.5
Drop slides where needed

Notes Page View

A great way to work with notes in PowerPoint is to take advantage of the Notes pane in the lower portion of the workspace. Sometimes, however, it's even easier to write and edit your notes by using a full page format. The Notes Page view gives you that option.

In this view, you can still see a miniature picture of your slide, but below that is a large space to write text, as in Figure 3.6. Just click within that space and begin typing your notes. When you switch back to Normal view, the notes will appear in the Notes pane.

Slide Show View

When you use the Slide Show view, you're actually running your presentation so that you can see it in the same way as your audience will. It's a full-screen view of your presentation, and each slide will appear as you have designated it should, either

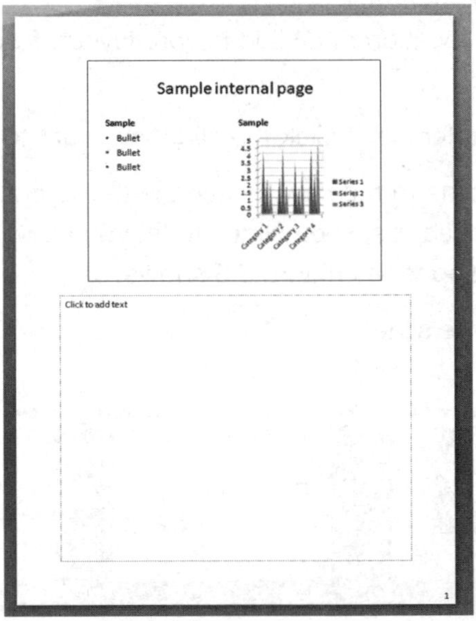

Figure 3.6
Notes Page view

through an automatic transition or by clicking through the slides manually.

This gives you the opportunity to make adjustments to timing, animations, graphics, transitions and other aspects of your presentation. For example, you might discover that an item you thought was moved off a slide is actually still showing when the presentation runs.

Although you can't physically make changes as the slide show runs in this view, you can quickly stop the presentation to make adjustments by clicking **Escape** on your keyboard.

→ Using the Outline Tab

In Chapter 2, you learned about the key workspace areas in PowerPoint. Another tool that can be used is the Outline tab, which is in the left pane behind the Slides tab, as Figure 3.7 shows.

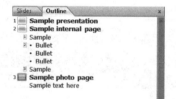

Figure 3.7
The Outline tab

The Outline tab helps you outline your presentation before you work on the layout. You can record information directly into the Outline tab by typing in it, but the tab will also record the information from each of your slides. So, if you prefer to lay out your slides, you can check the Outline tab occasionally to make sure your slides are flowing correctly.

If you want to see the outline for your presentation, just click the **Outline** tab. You can widen or narrow the pane by clicking the right-hand border and dragging the pane to the desired width.

Timesaver tip

In the Outline tab, the slide you have selected in your presentation will be highlighted. As you read through the outline, the highlight makes it easy to see which page you were working on before you switched to the Outline tab.

→ Changing the Default View of Your Presentation

You can set PowerPoint to open in a different view from Normal if you like. For example, if you prefer to work in Slide Sorter view, you can change the PowerPoint default so that all your presentations open in that view.

Your choices for default views include several different variations of Normal view, along with Slide Sorter, Outline Only and Notes. To change the default view in PowerPoint, follow these steps:

1. Click the **Microsoft Office** button.

2. Click **PowerPoint Options**.

3 In the Display section, click the dropdown arrow next to Open all documents using this view, shown in Figure 3.8.

4 Select the new view you want.

5 Click **OK**.

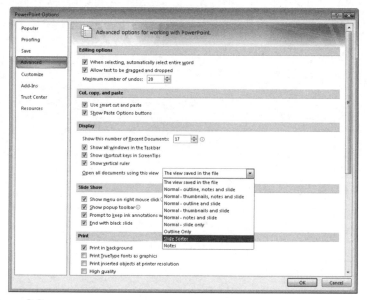

Figure 3.8
Change the default view in PowerPoint Options

4

Working with the Master Views

In this chapter, you will learn how to work with the Slide, Handout and Notes Masters available in PowerPoint 2007.

Master views allow you to change the look and feel of your presentation quickly and easily. There are several different masters that can be used in PowerPoint 2007. The one you will probably use most often is the Slide Master.

Slide Master lets you make changes to a single slide (the "master") and then have those changes applied universally throughout your presentation.

For example, if you want to use a specific header style on all your slides, you can apply the style to a Slide Master instead of going to individual slides in a presentation and applying the style separately to each. Or perhaps you want to include the date and presentation title on every footer in your presentation – input the information on the Slide Master and then forget about it. Newly added pages will automatically include any information you have placed on the Slide Master.

Jargon buster

Slide Master This is part of a template that stores information by using placeholders. Slide Masters are saved as single template files (*.potx).

When you customise a Slide Master, you can use it within a single presentation or you can save it as a PowerPoint presentation of its own so it can be used later. You can also use multiple Slide Masters within a single presentation so that different sections of your presentation can have special aspects where you want them, such as new backgrounds and text styles. Or, if you prefer, use a single Slide Master that contains multiple layouts.

Layouts are used as part of a Slide Master to position placeholders or information for instant use when a slide is used. For example, you might want to have a layout on a slide that directs users of a template to enter specific information. Or you might want to be sure the date and time appear on every page of a presentation. Maybe you want a specific type of layout to have a specific background colour. Changes to slide layouts can accomplish these things for you.

There are five built-in layouts in PowerPoint 2007, or you can customise your own. Any layout can include some or all of the following elements:

- Background objects
- Background fill (colour or picture)
- Title placeholder
- Subtitle placeholder
- Body placeholder, which can be a text box, chart, picture or graph
- Placeholder formatting, such as bullets
- Headers and footers.

Timesaver tip

Create Slide Masters before you create individual slides in your presentation. All slides added to your presentation will be based on the master, so it's easiest to create the Slide Master first.

→ Creating and Using the Slide Master

Slide Masters aren't difficult to create, but do take your time as you walk through the process. Before you follow the steps here, read through this chapter to be sure you understand all the options you have when using a Slide Master.

To create a Slide Master, follow these steps:

1 In a blank presentation, go to the **View** tab.

2 Click **Slide Master** in the Presentation Views group, as shown in Figure 4.1. A blank Slide Master will appear in the workspace. Note that the Slide and Outline tabs have been replaced with a grouping of slides with a master slide and multiple layout slides (also known as the master layout), as shown in Figure 4.2. This is called the Thumbnail pane.

Figure 4.1
The Slide Master command

Figure 4.2
In the Slide Master view, the Slide and Outline tabs in the left pane are replaced by the Thumbnail pane.

3 Click the **Microsoft Office** button.

4 Click **Save As**.

5 Type in a file name for the master slide layout, or accept the suggested file name.

6 Click **PowerPoint Template (*.potx)** in the Save As Type list. Note: leave the default location (Templates).

7 Click **Save**.

8 Go to the **Slide Master** tab and click **Close Master View** in the Close group.

> **Important**
>
> All of the remaining instructions for Slide Masters in this chapter assume you have opened your presentation in the Slide Master view.

Removing Unwanted Slides

To remove an unwanted slide from the master layout, follow these steps:

1 Right-click the slide in the Thumbnail pane. Click **Delete Layout** on the shortcut menu, shown in Figure 4.3. Repeat this step for each slide you want removed from the master layout.

Figure 4.3
The Delete Layout command

Removing Unwanted Placeholders

To remove a placeholder on a specific slide in the master layout, follow these steps:

1 Click the slide that contains the placeholders to be removed. In the Slide pane, click the border of the placeholder to be removed. Press **Delete** on your keyboard. Repeat this step for each placeholder that needs to be removed.

Adding New Placeholders

To add a placeholder to the master layout, follow these steps:

1 Click the slide that you want to contain the placeholder.

2 Go to the **Slide Master** tab and click **Insert Placeholder** in the Master Layout, as Figure 4.4 shows.

3 Click the placeholder type that you want to add to the slide.

4 Click the slide in the location where you want to add the placeholder.

Figure 4.4
Insert Placeholder menu options

5 Drag your cursor to draw the placeholder.

6 Release the cursor to finalise the placement.

Adding Custom Text to a Placeholder

To add custom text to single or multiple slide layouts, follow these steps:

1 Click the slide that will hold the customised text.

2 In the text placeholder, type in the custom text. For example, you might want your slide to say "Add Product Names Here" so that others using the template know where to input product information.

3 Go to the **Slide Master** tab. Click **Close Master View** in the Close group.

4 Go to the **Home** tab.

5 Click **Layout** in the Slides group.

6 Click the slide layout with the custom text. PowerPoint will automatically add it to your presentation.

Adding a Theme

To add a theme to your Slide Master, follow these steps:

1 Go to the **Slide Master** tab.

2 Click **Themes** in the Edit Theme group.

3 Click the desired theme, as shown in Figure 4.5.

Modifying the Background

To modify a background, follow these steps:

1 Go to the **Slide Master** tab.

2 Click **Background Styles** in the Background group.

3 Click the desired background, as shown in Figure 4.6.

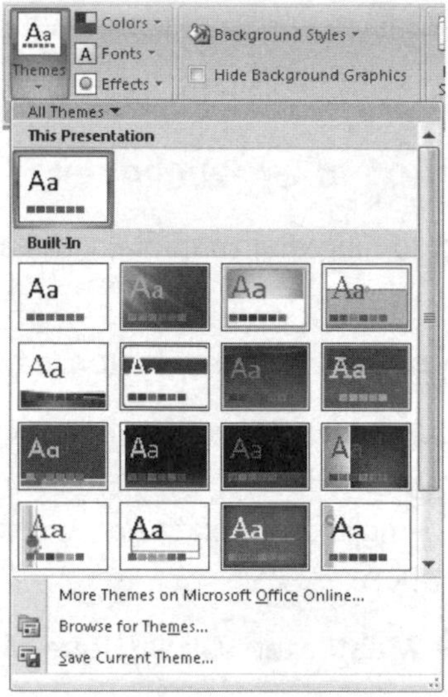

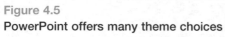

Figure 4.5
PowerPoint offers many theme choices

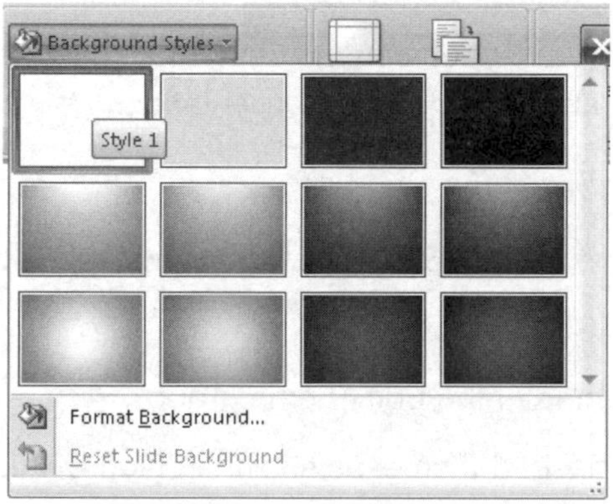

Figure 4.6
A variety of background styles are available

Setting Page Orientation

To set page orientation for slides in the master layout, follow these steps:

1 Go to the **Slide Master** tab.

2 Click **Slide Orientation** in the Page Setup group.

3 Click Portrait or Landscape, as shown in Figure 4.7.

Adding Custom Text to Slide Footers

To add text that will appear in all page footers in your presentation, follow these steps:

1 Go to the **Insert** tab.

2 Click **Header & Footer** in the Text group.

3 In the Header and Footer dialogue box, place a checkmark next to Footer, as Figure 4.8 shows.

Figure 4.7
The Slide Orientation command

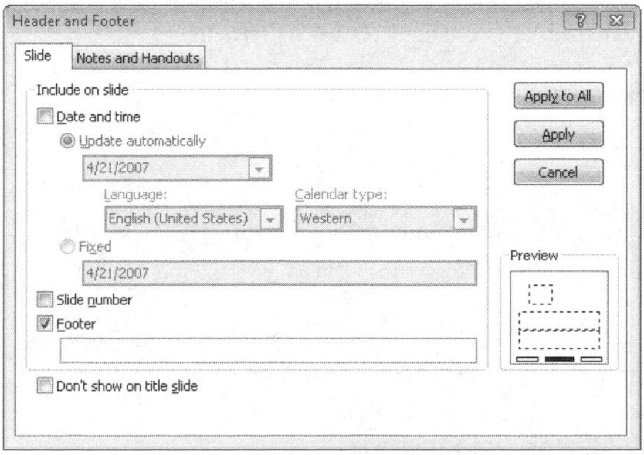

Figure 4.8
The Header and Footer dialogue box

4 In the blank text box beneath Footer, enter the custom text for your footers. This text will appear in the bottom centre of the slide.

5 Click **Apply to All**.

Renaming a Slide Master

If you need to rename a Slide Master, follow these steps:

1 Click the Slide Master you want to rename.

2 Go to the **Slide Master** tab.

3 Click **Rename** in the Edit Master group.

4 In the Rename Master dialogue box, type in the new name in the Master Name box, as shown in Figure 4.9.

5 Click **Rename**.

Renaming a Slide Layout

If you want to rename a slide layout, follow these steps:

1 Click the slide layout you want to rename.

2 Go to the **Slide Master** tab.

3 Click **Rename** in the Edit Master group.

4 In the Rename Layout dialogue box, type in the new name in the Layout Name box, shown in Figure 4.10.

5 Click **Rename**.

Figure 4.9
The Rename Master dialogue box

Rename Layout	[?] [⊠]
Layout name:	Rename
Custom Layout	
	Cancel

Figure 4.10
The Rename Layout dialogue box

4

→ Using the Handout Master

When you give a presentation, it's often helpful for the audience to be able to follow it by using printed handouts that contain the slides from the presentation. This way, the audience can make notes about your presentation and easily reference the slides.

The handouts can show only the slides, or they can be formatted during printing both to show slides and to provide space for notes. The Handout Master can be used to make a variety of changes quickly. Any changes you make to the Handout Master will appear in the printed outline for the presentation too.

You can make the following changes to a Handout Master:

- Move, resize or format headers.
- Move, resize or format footers.
- Set page orientation.
- Specify the number of slides to print per page.

Figure 4.11 shows a default Handout Master, which includes a header, date, footer and page number, along with six slides on the page.

Opening the Handout Master

 Go to the **View** tab.

 Click **Handout Master** in the Presentation Views group.

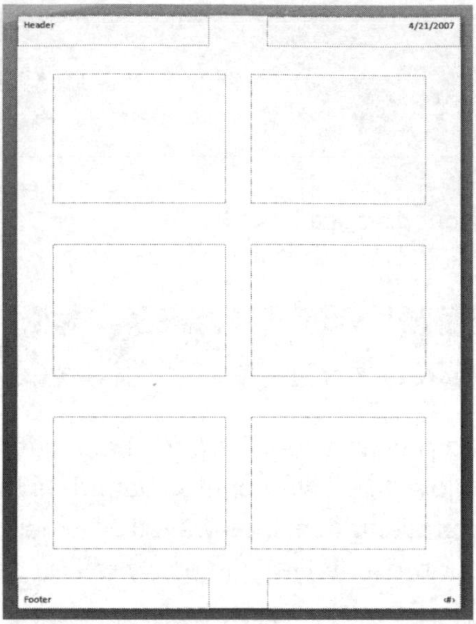

Figure 4.11
The Handout Master can be changed easily to suit your needs.

> ## Important
>
> When you have finished making changes to the Handout Master, click **Close Master View** in the Close group. All instructions in this section assume you are using the Handout Master view, unless otherwise noted.

Working with Handout Master Footers and Headers

The default Handout Master shows a header in the top left corner and a footer in the bottom left corner. To remove either or both, just uncheck the box next to Header or Footer in the Placeholders group.

To move a header or footer to a different location in the master, click its placeholder and drag it to the new location using the four-arrow handle, shown in Figure 4.12.

Enter text for the header or footer by clicking on the placeholder and typing directly into it.

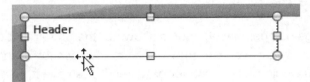

Figure 4.12
Header locations can be easily changed

Using the Date Feature

The date placeholder is shown in the upper left corner of the Handout Master. You can move it to another location in the same way you would move a header or footer.

To remove the date from the Handout Master, remove the checkmark from the Date box in the Placeholders group. You might prefer to use a different format for the date or to add the time along with the date. To do that, you will need to follow these steps:

1 Highlight the date on the Handout Master.

2 Keeping the Handout Master open, go to the **Insert** tab.

3 Click **Date & Time** in the Text group, as Figure 4.13 shows.

4 In the Date and Time dialogue box, select the new format you want to use. Your choices include date formats, time formats and date/time formats.

5 Place a checkmark in Update Automatically if you want to use that feature.

6 Click **OK**.

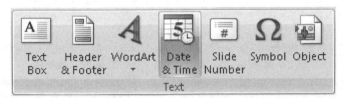

Figure 4.13
The Date & Time command

Using the Page Number Feature

The page number placeholder is shown at the bottom left of the Handout Master. You can move it to another location in the same way you would move a header or footer. To remove it, remove the checkmark in the box next to Page Number in the Placeholders group.

Timesaver tip

When you work with header, footer, date and/or page number placeholders in the Notes Master, you can make changes to them in the same way you would make changes while using the Handout Master.

→ Using the Notes Master

When you want to make formatting changes to your Notes pages, you need to use the Notes Master. Formatting changes can include font style, font colours, fill colour and more.

To open the Notes Master, follow these steps:

1 Go to the **View** tab.

2 Click **Notes Master** in the Presentation Views group.

Important

Remember: the Notes page shows you a miniature picture of the slide at the top of the page, so the Notes Master will show that as well. When you make changes, it's important to use the text placeholder in the lower portion of the Notes Master – you can't make changes to the slide picture.

Changing the Font

To change the font in the Notes Master, follow these steps:

1 Click the text placeholder.

2 Highlight the text you want to change.

3 Go to the **Home** tab.

4 Select the new font in the Font group, as shown in Figure 4.14.

Changing the Font Colour

To change the font colour in the Notes Master, follow these steps:

1 Click the text placeholder.

2 Highlight the text you want to change.

3 Go to the **Home** tab.

4 Select the new font colour in the Font group.

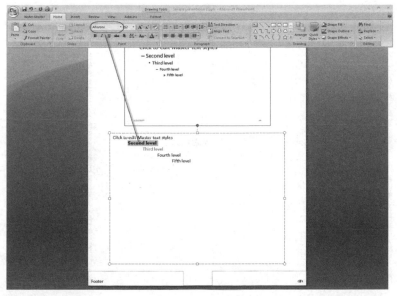

Figure 4.14
Fonts can be changed in the Notes Master

Changing the Font Size

To change the font size in the Notes Master, follow these steps:

1 Click the text placeholder.

2 Highlight the text you want to change.

3 Go to the **Home** tab.

4 Select the new font size in the Font group.

Aligning Text

To align text differently in the Notes Master, follow these steps:

1 Click the text placeholder.

2 Highlight the text you want to change.

3 Go to the **Home** tab.

4 Select the new alignment in the Paragraph group, as Figure 4.15 shows.

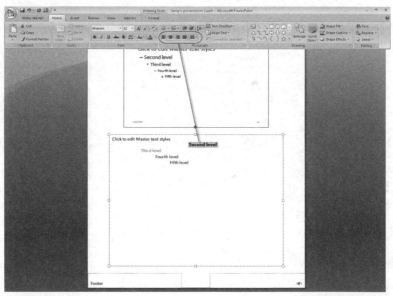

Figure 4.15
Font alignment commands

Timesaver tip

You can add logos and other art to the Notes and Handout Masters. Keep the appropriate master view open, and then go to the **Insert** tab and click **Picture** or **Clip Art**. Locate and select the artwork you want to add, and then position it where you want it. Pictures and objects added to Notes pages will not appear on the screen in Normal view.

4

5

Creating a Look for Your Presentation

In this chapter, you will learn how to work with colour schemes, use PowerPoint themes, apply design templates, work with background styles and use the Page Setup and Slide Orientation features.

→ Using Colour Schemes

When you create a presentation, it can be helpful to your audience if colours are used consistently throughout the slides. Jumping from one colour to another as each slide appears can be distracting to your audience.

PowerPoint 2007 has a wonderful array of colours from which to choose, called theme colours. When these colours are applied, the objects on the page instantly reflect the theme colour. For example, in Figure 5.1, you can see a sample page with a chart and a shape.

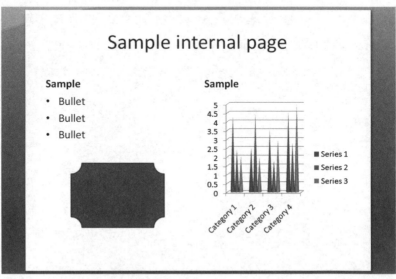

Figure 5.1
A slide using the Office colour scheme.

In the figure, both objects are shown in the Office colour scheme. The shape is blue and the chart is a mixture of blue, red and green.

In Figure 5.2, however, the scheme has been changed to the Opulent colour scheme. The shape is now bright pink; the chart is a mixture of bright pink, purple and orange. Try these themes yourself to see the difference in colour.

The change in the colours for both the chart and the shape was made instantly by using theme colours in PowerPoint. That's because when you apply a theme colour, the colours will flow throughout every object in your presentation. No matter which theme you have chosen for a presentation (this topic is covered in "Using Themes" later in this chapter), you can always modify the colour of the theme you've chosen by changing the theme colour.

Important

You can always change an individual object to another colour outside a scheme if you prefer, but using theme colours allows you to stay consistent throughout a presentation.

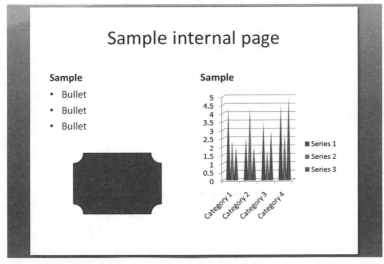

Figure 5.2
A slide using the Opulent colour scheme.

To use or change a theme colour in your presentation, follow these steps in Normal view:

1 From anywhere in the presentation, go to the **Design** tab.

2 Click **Colors** in the Themes group, as shown in Figure 5.3.

3 Select a colour theme. Notice that as you hover the cursor over different colour theme options, the colours on the slide on your screen change. This helps you to get an idea of how the new colour would look.

4 Click the colour theme to apply it to the presentation.

The presentation will automatically change colours on every slide as needed.

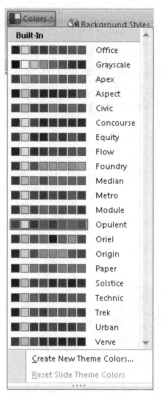

Figure 5.3
Available colour themes

5

→ Using Themes

By default, PowerPoint 2007 opens a blank presentation with a
blank slide. Sometimes, however, you may want to use colour
and effects through a presentation.

When you use a theme in your presentation, you can quickly
establish a style and tone for it. For example, if you want to
create a very businesslike tone, you can select a theme with
modern but subdued colours and effects. On the other hand, if
you want to establish a party atmosphere, you could select a
theme that uses bright colours and effects.

There are 20 built-in themes to choose from in PowerPoint 2007.
The Office theme is automatically applied to blank presentations,
but you can quickly change the look of your presentation by
following these steps to apply a built-in theme:

1 Go to the **Design** tab.

2 Click the **More** arrow in the Themes group, as shown in
Figure 5.4.

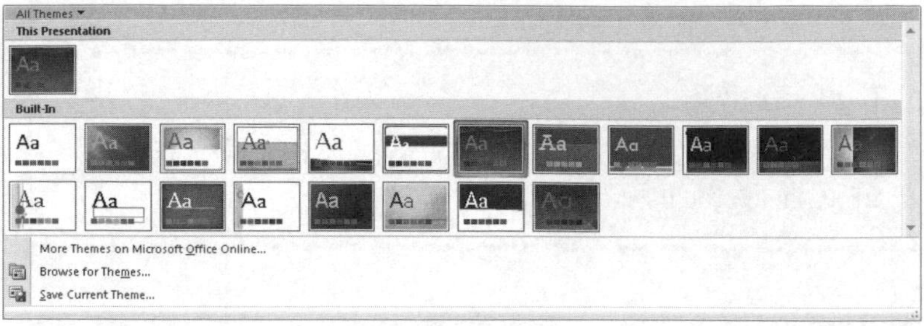

Figure 5.4
Use the More arrow to see the Theme QuickStyles Gallery.

3 From the QuickStyles Gallery, click the new theme desired.

The theme will be applied automatically throughout your presentation.

Timesaver tip

Preview a theme by hovering your cursor over it. Your current slide will change instantly so you can see how the theme will impact your content.

Customising a Theme

You can also customise themes by changing colours and fonts. This is a great idea if you like designing slides or if you like most aspects of a particular theme but want to modify it a bit.

Each theme colour is comprised of four text and background colours, six accent colours and two hyperlink colours. The possibilities for themes, however, are vast. By changing a colour here and there, for instance, you can quickly create your own themes that can be applied to a current or future presentation.

To create a new theme colour, follow these steps:

1 Go to the **Design** tab and click **Theme Colors** in the Themes group.

2 Click **Create New Theme Colors**, shown in Figure 5.5.

3 In the Create New Theme Colors dialogue box, click the button that corresponds to the change you want to make. For example, to change the colour of a followed hyperlink, click the button to the right of Followed Hyperlink, as shown in Figure 5.6.

4 In the colour menu that appears, select the new colour you want to use.

5 Repeat steps 3 and 4 for every colour change you want to make.

6 Type a name in the Name box for the new theme.

7 Click **Save**.

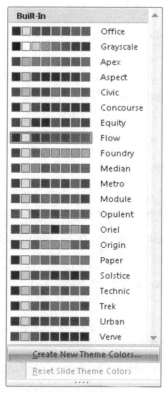

Figure 5.5
Create New Theme Colors command

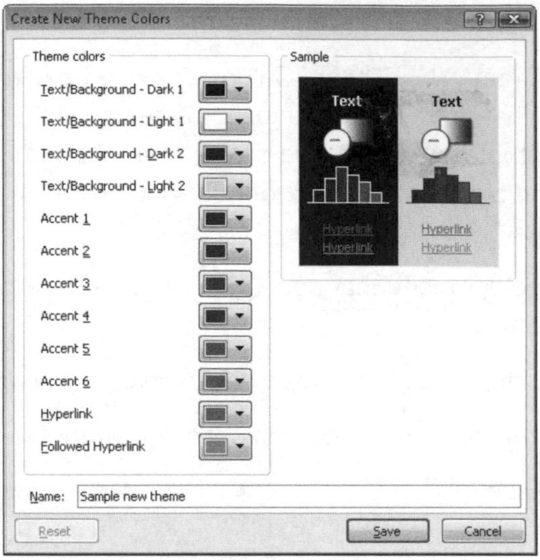

Figure 5.6
Create New Theme Colors dialogue box

Changes that you make during this process are reflected in the Sample section of the Create New Theme Colors dialogue box to help you see how the new theme will look.

To create a new theme font, follow these steps:

1 Go to the **Design** tab and click **Theme Fonts** in the Themes group.

2 Click **Create New Theme Fonts**, as Figure 5.7 shows.

3 In the Create New Theme Fonts dialogue box, select the new fonts for the heading and/or body, as shown in Figure 5.8.

4 Type in a new name for the theme font in the Name box.

5 Click **Save**.

Applying a Theme to a Single Slide

You can apply a theme to a single slide by following these steps:

1 In the Slide pane, open the slide where you want the theme changed.

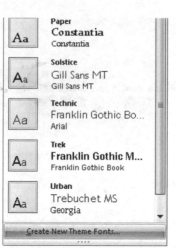

Figure 5.7
Create New Theme Fonts command

Figure 5.8
Name your new font

2 Go to the **Design** tab.

3 Click the **More** arrow in the Themes group.

4 Right-click the theme you want to apply.

5 In the dropdown menu, click **Apply To Selected Slides**, as Figure 5.9 shows.

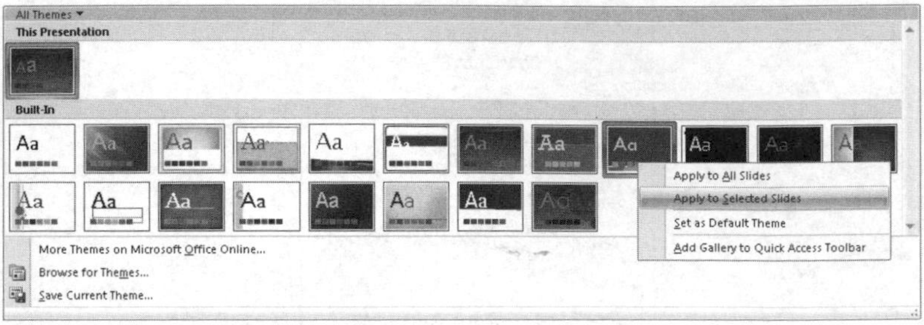

Figure 5.9
Apply a selected theme

Timesaver tip

Don't like the built-in themes and don't want to create your own? You can search for additional themes by clicking **More Themes on Microsoft Office Online** in the Theme QuickStyles Gallery.

→ Applying Design Templates

Microsoft Office Online offers a variety of templates, as mentioned in Chapter 2. There are additional template options available online called Design Templates that you might want to consider using if you aren't satisfied with the built-in themes or customisations you have created.

You can locate a design template by following these steps:

1 In PowerPoint, click **F1** to open PowerPoint Help.

2 In the Search box, type "Design Template".

3 Click your selection from the results options provided, shown in Figure 5.10.

4 On the Microsoft Office Online website, click **Download Now**, as Figure 5.11 shows.

Figure 5.10
An example of search results

5 The template will download to your computer and appear on your screen. Click the **Microsoft Office** button.

6 Click **Save As**.

7 Click **PowerPoint Presentation** (or another option if you prefer).

8 Save the presentation template to your desired location and as the type you prefer. If you save it to the Templates folder on your system, you will have easy access to the original template in the future. Don't forget to change its name if you wish.

9 Click **Save**.

Figure 5.11
An example template that can be downloaded

→ Working with Background Styles

Background styles are fun to work with, especially if you like to use your own creative juices when designing a presentation. Essentially, a background style is just a variation of a background fill on a slide. It is typically derived from a combination of theme colours and strengths. You can't change fonts or effects when you change a background fill.

5

To add a background style to your presentation, follow these steps:

1 Click the slide where you want the background style applied.

2 Go to the **Design** tab.

3 Click **Background Styles** in the Background group, shown in Figure 5.12.

4 Right-click the new background style you prefer.

- Click **Apply to All Slides** if you want the background style applied throughout your presentation.

- Click **Apply to Selected Slides** if you want it applied only to the slide(s) you have currently selected.

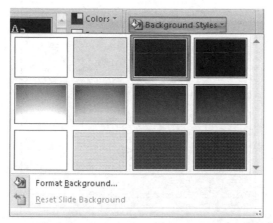

Figure 5.12
Background Styles menu

To add a background style to your presentation, follow these steps:

1 Click the slide where you want the background style applied.

2 Go to the **Design** tab.

3 Click **Background Styles** in the Background group.

4 Click **Format Background**.

5 In the Format Background dialogue box, click the options you want, as shown in Figure 5.13.

- If you select **Solid fill**, click the **Color** button to choose a colour. Then move the **Transparency** bar to the transparency level you prefer.

- If you select **Gradient fill**, you can choose from preset colours or create your own gradient using the options shown.

- If you select **Picture or texture fill**, you can insert a picture from your files or use clip art. You can also

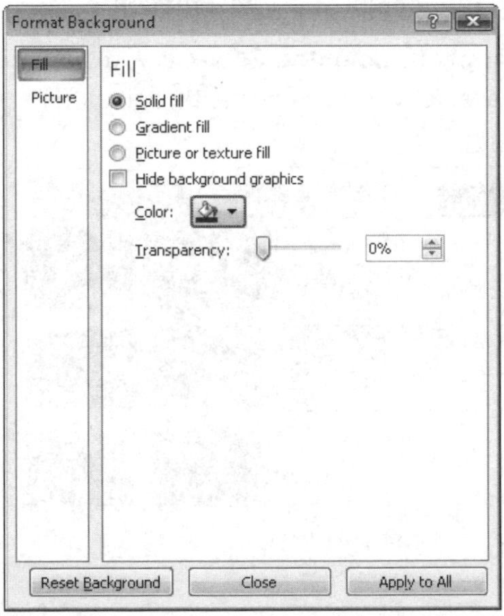

Figure 5.13
The Format Background dialogue box

designate whether the picture should be tiled, stipulate how it should be aligned, or choose other specifications.

■ To hide any background graphics that might be on your slide due to a theme, click **Hide background graphics**.

6 Click **Apply to All**.

7 Click **Close**.

→ Changing Slide Orientation

When you open a PowerPoint presentation, the slide layouts are shown in a horizontal or landscape orientation. Most people never change that because when the show is running in Slide Show mode, the entire screen is not filled by the slide.

However, there may be times when you want to use the portrait orientation for your presentation. To do that, follow these steps:

1 In an open presentation, go to the **Design** tab.

2 Click **Slide Orientation** in the Page Setup group.

3 Click **Portrait**.

All slides in the presentation will now be shown in portrait orientation. To change back to landscape orientation, follow steps 1 and 2 above and click **Landscape** instead of **Portrait** in step 3.

Although only one orientation can be used in a single presentation, there is a way to use both portrait and landscape orientations in what *seems* like a single presentation. To do this, you will need to create and then link together two presentations. As you show the first presentation, you click on a link at some point that goes to the second presentation. Then, in the second presentation, you can either finish the presentation or link back to the first presentation to finish.

Follow these steps to link together two presentations:

1 In the first presentation, select the text or object that you will use to link to the second presentation.

2 Go to the **Insert** tab.

3 Click **Action** in the Links group, as shown in Figure 5.14.

4 In the Action Settings dialogue box, decide whether you want the link to happen when you actually click the mouse or when you just hover the mouse over the link. Click the corresponding tab, as Figure 5.15 shows.

5 Select **Hyperlink to:** and then click **Other PowerPoint Presentation** from the dropdown menu.

6 In the Hyperlink to Other PowerPoint Presentation dialogue box, locate and select the second presentation.

7 Click **OK**.

8 In the Hyperlink to Slide dialogue box, select the slide you want to link to in the second presentation.

9 Click **OK**.

10 In the Action Settings dialogue box, click **OK**.

In the second presentation, repeat steps 1–10. Now both presentations will link together and you can jump between them easily.

Figure 5.14
The Action command

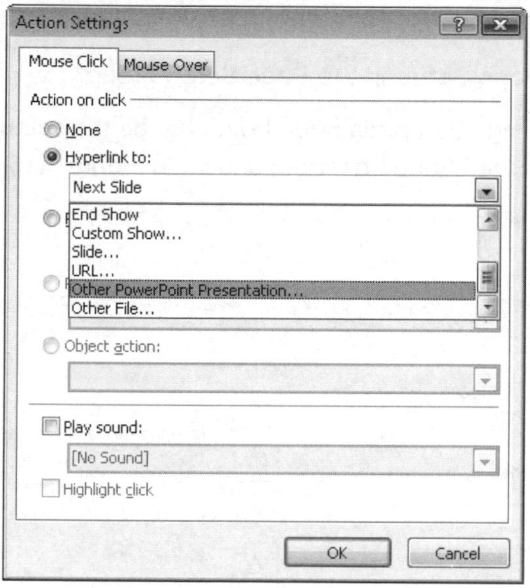

Figure 5.15
The Hyperlink command and menu

Timesaver tip

To remove a hyperlink quickly from a presentation, right-click the hyperlink in Normal view. Click **Remove Hyperlink** from the shortcut menu.

→ Modifying Page Setup

Slides are typically sized for on-screen computer shows (On-screen Show 4:3), but you might prefer to change that occasionally when you use different-sized screens. For example, you might be presenting in an auditorium that uses a large screen.

To modify the page setup for your presentation, follow these steps:

1 Go to the **Design** tab in an open presentation.

2 Click **Page Setup** in the Page Setup group.

3 In the Page Setup dialogue box, change the setting under Slides Sized For as desired, shown in Figure 5.16.

4 Click **OK**.

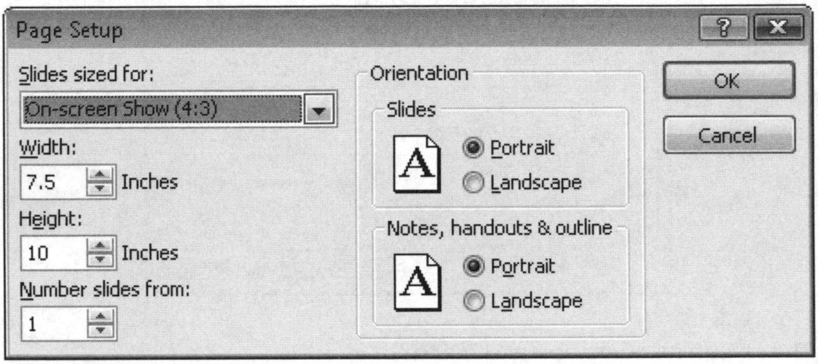

Figure 5.16
The Page Setup dialogue box

6

Creating Slide Text

In this chapter, you will learn how to work with text in your presentation. You'll discover how to make text boxes, work with fonts and text formats, use QuickStyles and create WordArt. Text is a huge part of a PowerPoint presentation. Add too little and your audience won't really understand your points; add too much and your audience will get lost in all the information. The trick, then, is to learn how to use PowerPoint text tools and functions so that you can communicate effectively with your audience.

→ Creating a Text Box

To add a simple text box to your presentation, follow these steps:

1 Go to the **Insert** tab.

2 Click **Text Box** in the Text group, as Figure 6.1 shows.

3 Click the slide in the Slide pane and drag the cursor to draw the text box.

4 Begin typing in the text box.

When a text box is drawn on a slide, PowerPoint intuitively moves to the Home tab so that you can take advantage of the text tools and functions located there. The most commonly used text tools related to font and paragraph functions are located in the Font and Paragraph groups on the Home tab, as shown in Figure 6.2.

The Font group includes the following commands:

- Font types
- Font sizes
- Font colours
- Bold, italic, underline and shadow

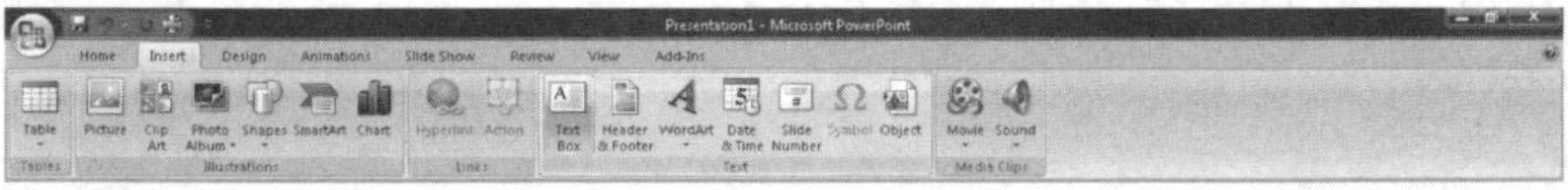

Figure 6.1
The Text Box command

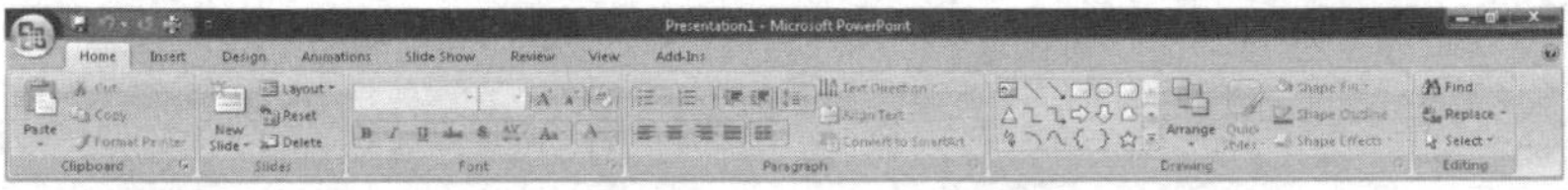

Figure 6.2
Text tools are located on the Home tab.

- Strikethrough

- Character spacing

- Change case

- Clear all formatting

- Decrease/increase font size.

> **Important**
>
> When you work with text in PowerPoint, you'll sometimes notice a small "floating" menu near the text box on the slide, as shown in Figure 6.3. This is called the Mini Toolbar – it's a mini text menu that holds several font and paragraph commands. It will stay translucent in the background unless you click it to use a command, and it will disappear when you move to a different area of a slide.

The Paragraph group includes the following commands:

- Alignment options

- Columns

- Line spacing

- List levels

- Bullet options

- Text direction

- Text alignment

- SmartArt options.

Figure 6.3

A floating menu allows you to access a variety of text commands directly from a slide.

→ Working with Fonts

It's fun to play with fonts in PowerPoint, but be sure your font choices don't overpower your message. There are lots of ways you can work with fonts, but it's a good idea to keep different fonts and font options to a minimum to help your audience concentrate on your message.

Adding Bold, Italic and Underlining to Text

For emphasis, you can add bold, italics and underlining to text in your presentation. To do that, follow these steps:

1 Highlight the text you want to change.

2 Go to the **Home** tab.

3 In the Font group, click the **Bold**, **Italics** or **Underline** option, shown in Figure 6.4.

If you need to remove bold, italics or underlining from a word or phrase, follow the steps above. Clicking the option a second time removes the formatting.

Adding a Shadow to Text

To add a shadow to selected text, follow these steps:

1 Highlight the text.

2 Go to the **Home** tab.

3 Click **Shadow** in the Font group, as Figure 6.5 shows.

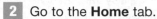

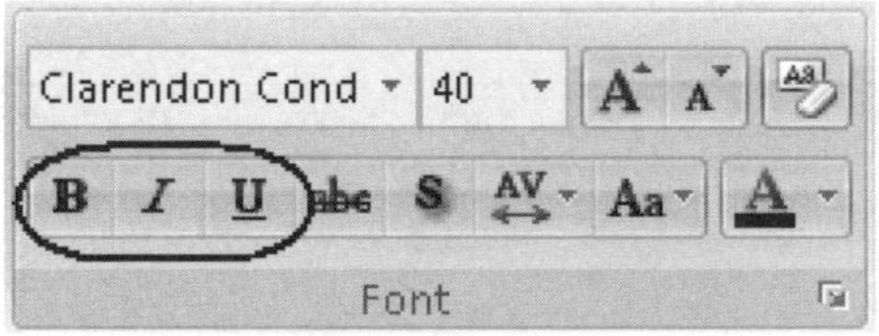

Figure 6.4
Bold, Italics and Underline commands

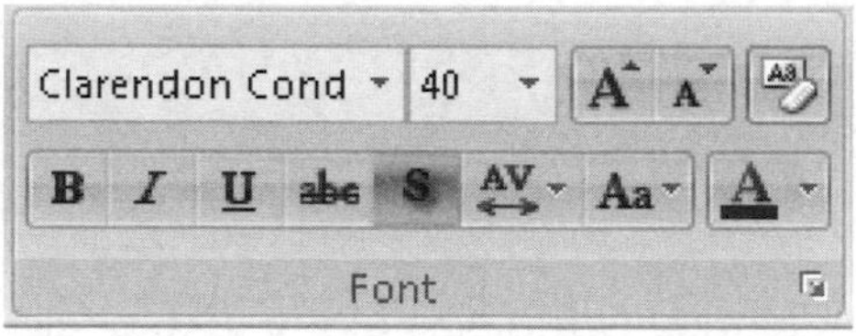

Editing Text by Using Strikethrough

6

In PowerPoint, there are no options to track changes when edits are made to text. That makes it difficult to see where someone might have changed text in your presentation. If you ask someone to edit your presentation – or if you edit someone else's – changes can be made using the Strikethrough feature. This option places a line through the centre of the text so that it's obvious the text is being changed or deleted, as shown in Figure 6.6. When an edit is accepted, just delete the entire word.

To place a strikethrough in a word or phrase, follow these steps:

1 Highlight the word or phrase.

2 Go to the **Home** tab.

3 Click **Strikethrough** in the Font group, as Figure 6.7 shows.

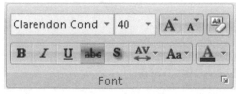

~~Sample~~ text

Figure 6.6
An example of Strikethrough

Figure 6.7
The Strikethrough command

→ Working with Text Size, Alignment and Spacing

When you want to modify the size of the text, or align or space it differently, you can use the tools in the Paragraph group of the Home tab.

Changing Text Size

Text size is often changed to be certain that audience members can see the text in a large auditorium, but it's a good idea to stay between 14 and 20 point for most presentations.

To change text size, follow these steps:

1 Highlight the text.

2 Go to the **Home** tab.

3 Click the down arrow in the Font size box of the Font group, as shown in Figure 6.8.

- Notice that as you hover the cursor over different font size options, the font size you have selected on your slide automatically changes to show you how the new size will look.

4 Select the new font size.

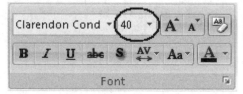

Figure 6.8
The Font Size command

Changing Text Alignment

To change text alignment so that it is aligned left, centre, right or justified in the text box, follow these steps:

1 Click the text box.

2 Go to the **Home** tab.

3 Click the alignment you prefer from the alignment options of the Paragraph group, shown in Figure 6.9.

To change text alignment so that it is aligned top, middle or bottom in the text box, follow these steps:

1 Click the text box.

2 Go to the **Home** tab.

3 Click **Align Text** in the Paragraph group.

4 Using the dropdown menu, click the alignment option you prefer, as shown in Figure 6.10.

Figure 6.9
Text Alignment options

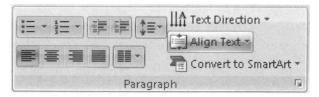

Figure 6.10
The Align Text command

Changing Line Spacing

If you need to squeeze a little more text on to a slide, or change the spacing between lines, you might want to modify the line spacing within a text box. To change line spacing, follow these steps:

1 Click the text box.

2 Go to the **Home** tab.

3 Click **Line Spacing**.

4 Click the spacing option you prefer, as Figure 6.11 shows.

In Figure 6.12, you can see how changing line spacing makes text look very different.

Figure 6.11
The Line Spacing command

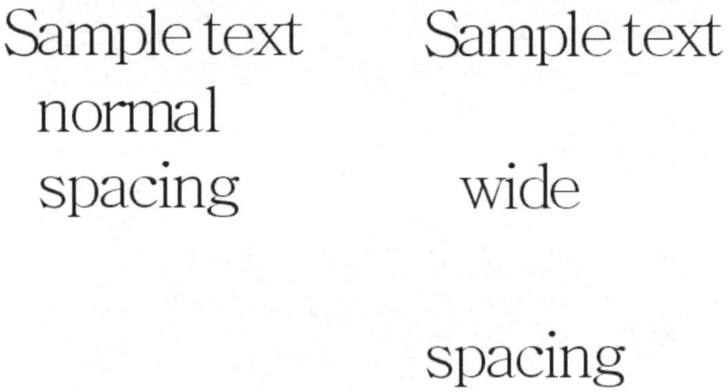

Sample text
normal
spacing

Sample text

wide

spacing

Figure 6.12
You can change the spacing in a line to make it very wide or very close together.

Changing Character Spacing

Sometimes changing the spacing between the characters in a word or sentence can help with spacing issues on a slide. To change character spacing, follow these steps:

1 Highlight the text.

2 Go to the **Home** tab.

3 In the Font group, click **Character Spacing**, as shown in Figure 6.13.

> **Timesaver tip**
>
> You can rotate a text box quickly by clicking the box and then grabbing the green handle and using your mouse to rotate the text box to the new position.

6

Changing Sentence Case

When you copy text into a presentation, sometimes it's not always in the correct case. For example, text might appear in lower case ("hi, my name is joe") when it should be in both lower and upper case ("Hi, my name is Joe"). You can change the case of a sentence quickly using the Sentence Case command. To do that, follow these steps:

1 Highlight the text.

2 Go to the **Home** tab.

3 Click **Change Case**, shown in Figure 6.14.

4 Click the new sentence case you prefer, as Figure 6.15 shows.

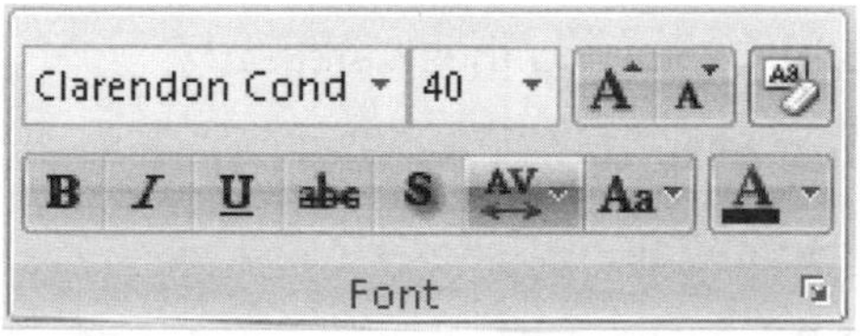

Clarendon Cond ▾ 40 ▾ A˄ A˅ Aa
B *I* U̲ a̶b̶c̶ S AV Aa˅ A˅
Font

Figure 6.13
The Character Spacing command

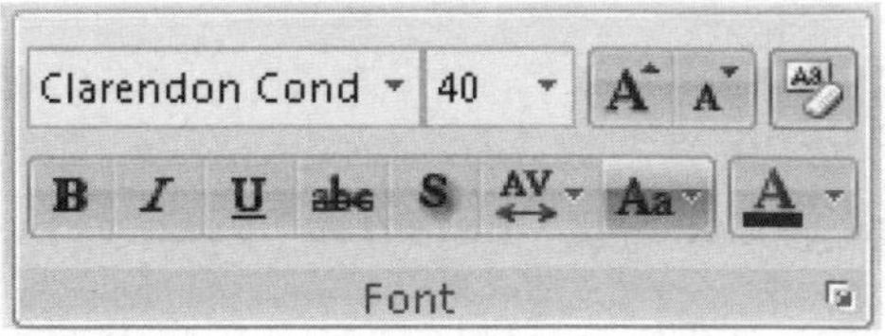

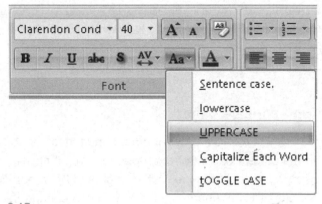

Figure 6.14
The Change Case command

Figure 6.15
Sentence Case options

→ Changing Text Direction

Text boxes will automatically show text in a standard, left-to-right reading format for languages that use this kind of reading format. However, you might want to dress up a slide by changing the direction of the text.

You can do that by following these steps:

1 Click the text box.

2 Go to the **Home** tab.

3 Click **Text Direction** in the Paragraph group, as shown in Figure 6.16.

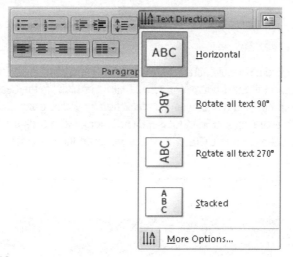

Figure 6.16
Text Direction menu options

4 Click one of the menu options.

5 Use the text box handles to pull the text box to the size needed for the new text direction if necessary, as Figure 6.17 shows.

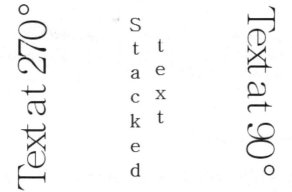

Figure 6.17
Place text wherever you need to

Timesaver tip

Need to find a special character such as a degree symbol? In Windows Vista, go to the **Start** button and type "Character Map" in the Search box. Click the program to open it. Select the font you're using, then click the character you want to use. Click **Select**. Move back to PowerPoint and enter **CTRL** + **V** where you want the character inserted.

→ Adding Colour, Outline and Effects to Text

Text boxes can be a bit boring. If you want to spice up yours, try adding colour, an outline or an effect.

To add colour to a text box, follow these steps:

1 Click the text box.

2 Go to the **Format** tab under Drawing Tools.

3 In the Shape Styles group, click **Shape Fill**, as shown in Figure 6.18.

4 Click the new colour for the text box.

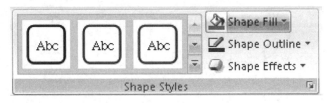

Figure 6.18
The Shape Fill command

You can also add pictures, textures and gradient colours to the text box by selecting those options instead during step 4 above.

To add an outline to a text box, follow these steps:

1 Click the text box.

2 Go to the **Format** tab under Drawing Tools.

3 In the Shape Styles group, click **Shape Outline**, shown in Figure 6.19.

4 Click a colour for the outline.

You can also make the outline heavier or lighter by selecting the **Weight** option in step 4. Or, if you prefer, turn the outline into a dashed line by selecting **Dashes** in step 4.

To add effects to a text box, follow these steps:

1 Click the text box.

2 Go to the **Format** tab under Drawing Tools.

3 In the Shape Styles group, click **Effects**.

4 From the menu, select the effect you want. Your text will appear something similar to Figure 6.20, depending on the effects you've chosen.

Figure 6.19
The Shape Outline command

Figure 6.20
A sample text box with three-dimensional and bevel effects applied.

→ Using QuickStyles

In PowerPoint, QuickStyle Galleries offer you multiple design options in just a click or two of the mouse. When you work with text, there are three key QuickStyle Galleries that you will want to become familiar with. All are located on the Format tab under Drawing Tools, which becomes active when you click a text box.

The Shapes Gallery

The first QuickStyles Gallery to experiment with is the Shapes gallery. In this gallery, you have the option of turning a simple text box into a multitude of shapes such as arrows, circles, callouts and stars. By default, a text box will appear in a rectangle format, although borders are not shown. To use shapes, you first need to format the text box so that its borders appear; then you use the Shapes gallery to select a new shape.

To format the text box so that its borders are visible, follow these steps:

1 Right-click the text box.

2 Click **Format Shape** on the shortcut menu, as shown in Figure 6.21.

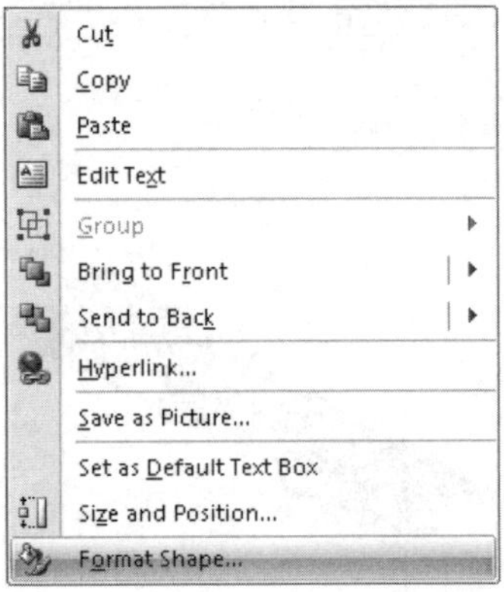

Figure 6.21
The Format Shape command

3 In the Format Shape dialogue box, click **Line Color** in the left pane.

4 Click **Solid Line** in the right pane, as Figure 6.22 shows.

5 Click a different colour if you wish.

6 Click a transparency percentage if you wish.

7 Click **Close**.

To apply a shape to an existing text box from the Shapes gallery, follow these steps:

1 Click the text box.

2 Go to the **Format** tab under Drawing Tools.

3 Click **Edit Shape** in the Insert Shapes group.

4 Hover the cursor over Change Shape.

5 When the full gallery appears, as shown in Figure 6.23, click the shape you want to use.

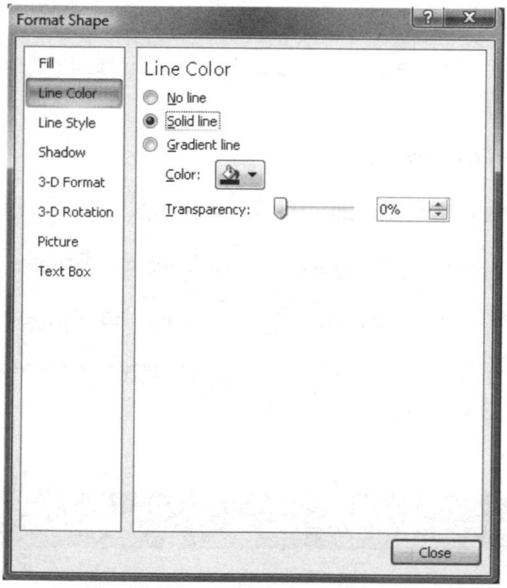

Figure 6.22
The Solid Line command

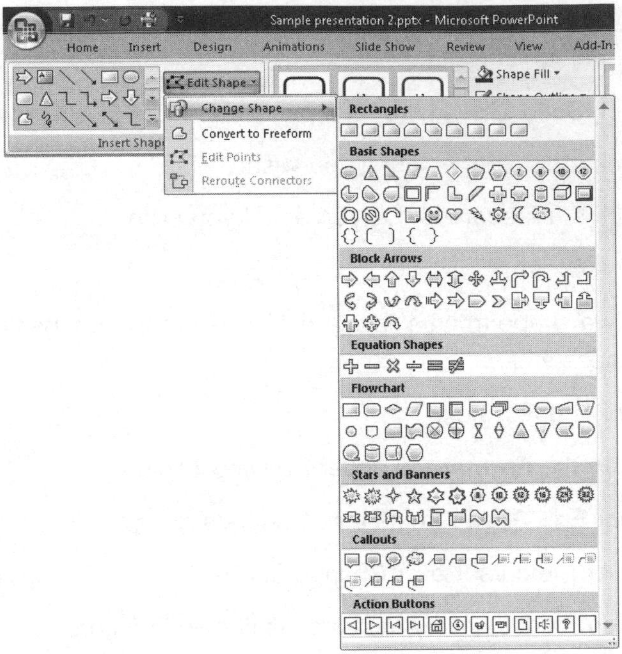

Figure 6.23
With the Shapes gallery, you can turn text boxes into fun new shapes.

If you prefer to create a text box using a shape first, follow these steps:

1 Go to the **Insert** tab.

2 Click **Shapes** in the Illustrations group.

3 Click the shape you want to use from the Shapes gallery.

4 Drag your cursor on the slide to draw the shape.

5 Begin typing. Your text will appear within the shape, as Figure 6.24 shows.

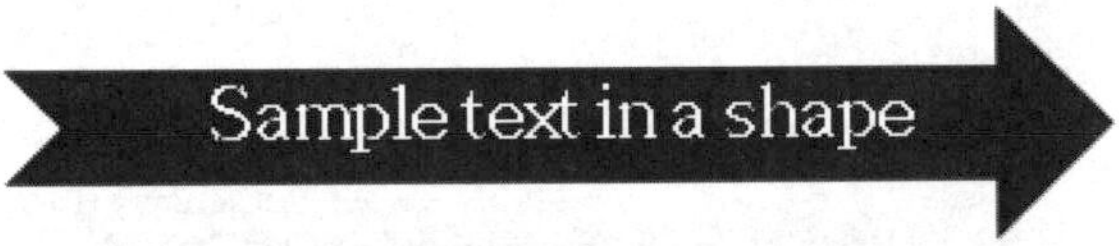

Sample text in a shape

Figure 6.24
Sample text in a shape

> ### Timesaver tip
> You can format text within a shape the same way you would format it in a regular text box.

The Shape Styles Gallery

A second gallery to become familiar with is the Shape Styles gallery. Once you have created a text box and applied the shape to it that you want, you can quickly change the text box into a style you like. Figure 6.25 shows you the difference that can be achieved by using the Shape Styles gallery.

To change a text box shape using the Shape Styles gallery, follow these steps:

1 Click the text box shape.

2 Go to the **Format** tab under Drawing Tools.

3 Click the **More** arrow in the Shape Styles gallery.

4 Click the new style you want for the shape. You can preview the styles by hovering the cursor over the new style and watching how it changes the shape on the slide.

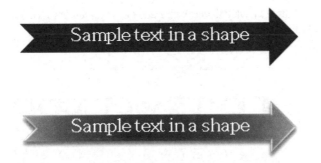

Figure 6.25
The text box shape at the top shows what the shape looks like before using the Shape Styles gallery. The one on the bottom shows what the same shape looks like after using the gallery.

The WordArt Gallery

Probably the most fun you'll have playing with text options will come when you use the WordArt tool. WordArt is really a gallery of text styles that can be added to your presentation for decorative purposes. You can add WordArt by creating it directly or by applying it to existing text.

To create WordArt, follow these steps:

1 Go to the **Insert** tab.

2 Click **WordArt** in the Text group.

3 Click a style in the WordArt menu.

4 Type in your text. Your sample might look similar to the one shown in Figure 6.26.

YOUR TEXT HERE

Figure 6.26
A WordArt sample.

To change a current text box into WordArt, follow these steps:

1 Highlight the text you want changed.

2 Go to the **Format** tab under Drawing Tools.

3 Click the **More** arrow to display the WordArt Style gallery.

4 Click the WordArt style you prefer.

Timesaver tip

You can apply WordArt to the text within a shape. The shape will not change: only the text changes.

7

Working with Graphics

In this chapter, you will learn how to use graphics in a presentation, explore how to add pictures and clip art, use shapes and SmartArt, add charts and use a variety of picture tools to make your graphics look as professional as possible.

→ Understanding how Graphics are Used in a Presentation

For most people, adding graphics to a PowerPoint presentation means adding pictures or clip art. It's a great way to include a little interest in a slide. The most important thing to remember when you use any kind of graphic in a presentation is to be certain that it complements the text. Pictures and other graphics can easily overpower the message you're trying to send, so be judicious when using graphics of any kind.

Slide layouts usually offer good options for placement of graphics. You can always paste graphics into your presentation and resize them by using the handles, but this process can sometimes cause pixelisation; that means your graphic might not be as crisp and clear as it could be. To avoid this problem, save graphics to your hard drive whenever possible; then resize the graphic to the size you need using a graphics program.

→ Adding Pictures

When you want to add a picture to a presentation, follow these steps:

1. Open your presentation so that the slide where the picture or clip art will be placed is open in the slide pane.

2. Go to the **Insert** tab, as shown in Figure 7.1.

3. Click **Picture** in the Illustrations group.

4. Locate and select the picture in the Insert Picture dialogue box.

5. Click **Insert**.

After the picture is placed on the slide, you will have a new tab on the Ribbon. That's because PowerPoint will launch a Picture

Figure 7.1
The Insert Picture command

Tools tab that then displays the Format tab. You will use this tab to perform most of the actions needed to customise the picture to your liking.

For example, 28 picture styles and dozens of picture shapes are available, plus you can crop a picture, add borders, and make other changes using the Format tab.

> **Important**
>
> If you move to a different area of the slide, the Picture Tools tab will disappear. It only becomes accessible to you when you have selected the actual picture you want to work on.

→ The Adjust Group

You'll find that you will work often with the Adjust group on the Format tab. This group is useful for ensuring your picture retains good quality. Six tools are accessible in this group: Brightness, Contrast, Recolor, Compress Pictures, Change Picture and Reset Picture.

Brightness

To improve a picture's clarity, you can increase or decrease the brightness of the picture. Follow these steps to change the brightness of a picture:

1 Click the picture.

2 Go to the **Format** tab.

3 Click **Brightness** in the Adjust group.

4 Select the brightness percentage you prefer, as Figure 7.2 shows.

Contrast

Use the Contrast tool to increase or decrease the contrast in the picture. This makes details stand out or fade away. To apply the contrast tool to a picture, follow these steps:

1 Click the picture.

2 Go to the **Format** tab.

3 Click **Contrast** in the Adjust group.

4 Select the contrast percentage you prefer, as shown in Figure 7.3.

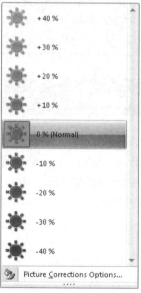

Figure 7.2
The Brightness Percentages menu

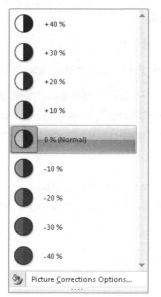

Figure 7.3
The Contrast Percentages menu

Recolor

The Recolor tool will help you add style to your picture. This option allows you to recolour with selected colour modes, use dark or light variations, or transform the picture to a transparency. To use the Recolor tool, follow these steps:

1 Click the picture.

2 Go to the **Format** tab.

3 Click **Recolor** in the Adjust group.

4 Select the colour mode or variation you prefer, as in Figure 7.4.

Compress Pictures

This tool will compress the size of your picture in the presentation. This allows you to see the compression size based on the target output (print, screen or e-mail). To use the Compress Pictures tool, follow these steps:

1 Click the picture.

2 Go to the **Format** tab.

3 Click **Compress Pictures** in the Adjust group.

4 In the Compress Pictures dialogue box, select **Apply to selected pictures only** if you do not want the compression applied to all pictures in the presentation (see Figure 7.5).

5 Click **Options**.

6 In the Compression Settings dialogue box, place a checkmark next to the Compression Options you prefer.

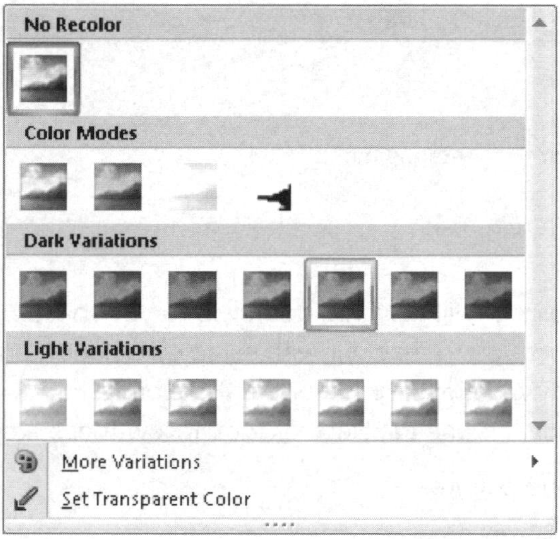

Figure 7.4
The Recolor menu

Figure 7.5
The Compress Pictures dialogue box

7 Select a target output.

8 Click **OK**.

9 In the Compress Pictures dialogue box, click **OK**.

Change Picture

To change a picture quickly without returning to the Insert tab, follow these steps:

1 Click the picture.

2 Go to the **Format** tab.

3 Click **Change Picture** in the Adjust group.

4 In the Insert Picture dialogue box, locate and select the new picture you want to use.

5 Click **Insert**.

Reset Picture

When you need to return a picture to its original shape and size, follow these steps:

1 Click the picture.

2 Go to the **Format** tab.

3 Click **Reset Picture** in the Adjust group.

> **Important**
>
> Using the Reset Picture option will return the photo to its original size from your hard drive, not the size it was when you first placed it into PowerPoint. Typically, when you insert a picture into PowerPoint, the picture will appear in the size of a particular picture box or even the size of the full slide. Reset Picture, however, resets the picture to the size it is when you access it directly from your hard drive.

→ The Picture Styles Group

The other group you'll work with often is the Picture Styles group. This group has a variety of tools available to help you turn your pictures into pieces of art.

The Picture Styles QuickStyle Gallery

The Picture Styles QuickStyle Gallery lets you change the framing and perspective of your picture. Take a few minutes to play with this gallery – you'll have some fun as you learn about the different picture styles available.

To work with the Picture Styles QuickStyle Gallery, follow these steps:

1 Click the picture.

2 Go to the **Format** tab.

3 Click the **More** button ⇡ in the Picture Styles group.

4 Click the style you prefer. The selections are shown in Figure 7.6.

As you hover your cursor over the Picture Style options, watch how the picture changes. This allows you to see how the picture will look with any given style.

Figure 7.6
There are many Picture Style selections to choose from.

Turning Pictures into Shapes

Another fun thing to do with pictures is to change the shape. With PowerPoint, you have dozens of shape options to choose from. For example, as shown in Figure 7.7, you can change a standard horizontal picture into a heart-shaped picture simply by selecting the heart shape with the Picture Shape tool.

With this tool, you can change the shape of the picture with a single click by choosing from primary options such as:

- Action buttons
- Basic shapes, such as circles and ovals

Figure 7.7
You can easily turn regular pictures into fun shapes.

- Block arrows
- Callouts
- Equation shapes
- Flowchart shapes
- Rectangles
- Stars and banners.

To change a picture's shape, follow these steps:

1 Click the picture.

2 Go to the **Format** tab.

3 Click **Picture Shape** in the Picture Styles group, and you'll see something like Figure 7.8.

4 Click the shape you prefer.

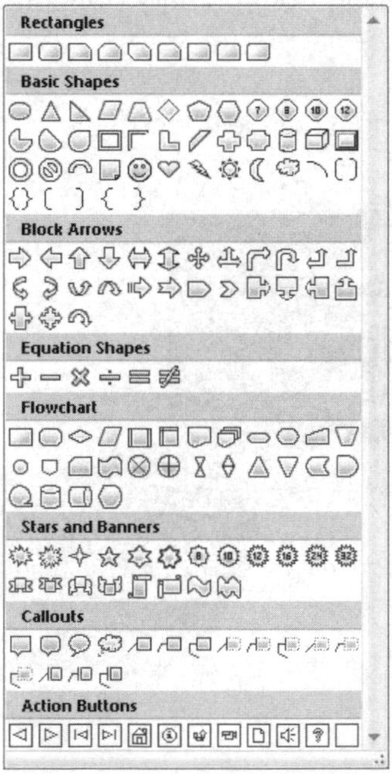

Figure 7.8
The Shapes menu

Changing a Picture Border

Once you have selected a style and shape for your picture, you can customise it further by changing the border. You can change colours, add weight to the border, or change a solid line to a dashed line.

To change a picture's border, follow these steps:

1 Click the picture.

2 Go to the **Format** tab.

3 Click **Picture Border** in the Picture Styles group.

4 Click the border you prefer, as shown in Figure 7.9.

7

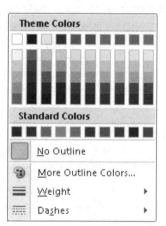

Figure 7.9
The Colors menu

 **→ The Arrange Group**

A third group, which you'll probably use less often than the others, is the Arrange group. This group holds the commands that allow you to place a picture in front of or behind another object and rotate your pictures to new angles. It also holds alignment options.

Placing a Picture in Front of or Behind another Object

When you use the Bring a Picture to the Front command, the picture will move to the front of all other objects on your slide. In contrast, the Bring Forward command merely moves the picture forward one step.

To change the placement of a picture so that it does this, follow these steps:

1 Click the picture.

2 Using the down arrow, click **Bring to Front** in the Arrange group on the Format tab.

3 Click **Bring to Front** or **Bring Forward**.

If you want to move a picture to a location behind other objects, you need to use the **Send to Back** command in the same group instead of the Bring to Front command.

Timesaver tip

You can group together multiple objects by pressing **CTRL** and clicking each object. Then go to the **Format** tab and click **Group** in the Arrange group. This command joins together multiple objects so that they are treated as a single item.

Using the Selection Pane

When you have several items on your slide that have been placed on top of one another, try using the Selection Pane to move them around if you decide on a new placement order. The Selection Pane will show all objects – including text shapes – on your slide, as shown in Figure 7.10. The objects are shown in the order they were placed on the slide.

To move an object in front of or behind another using the Selection Pane, follow these steps:

1 Decide which object needs to be moved. Click one object.

2 Go to the **Format** tab and click **Selection Pane**, as in Figure 7.11.

3 Click the blue **Up** or **Down** arrow at the bottom of the pane.

4 The corresponding object on the slide will move accordingly.

5 Continue to reorder shapes by repeating step 2 until you are finished.

6 Close the pane by clicking the **Close** button ✕ at the top right of the pane.

Figure 7.10
Items are easily moved in the Selection Pane using the up and down arrows.

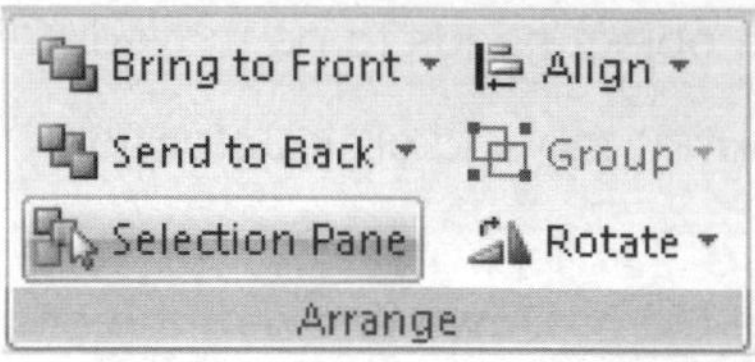

Figure 7.11
The Selection Pane command

> ## Important
>
> You can place multiple effects on to a picture, but keep your audience in mind as you do. Will the picture look as good on a 10-foot-high screen as it does on your computer monitor?

Using the Size Group

When you need to make changes to a specific picture, you can use the Size group. Five options – crop, height, width, size and position – are available here. These options allow you to remove unwanted portions of a picture, change the height or width of a picture, and resize/reposition the picture on your slide. You also have the option to display Web browser text as a picture loads if you will be posting your presentation on the Internet.

> ## Important
>
> If you need to download pictures for use in PowerPoint 2007, you need to download them to your hard drive first before you can insert them into your presentation. Although earlier versions of PowerPoint allowed you to download pictures directly into PowerPoint from your scanner or camera, that option is no longer available with PowerPoint 2007.

→ Adding Clip Art

You can insert a variety of clip art into your presentation, including drawings, movies, sounds and stock photography.

These items are usually stored in the Clip Organizer, which uses these four collections:

- **My Collections** – clips that you create and add to your own collection.

- **Office Collections** – clips that are offered with Microsoft Office 2007.

- **Shared Collections** – clips that are typically available on shared file servers or common workstations. Your network administrator must create and export the collection for use.

- **Web Collections** – clips that are available through the Microsoft Office Online collection. You need an active Internet connection to access these.

To add clip art to your presentation, follow these steps:

1 Open the slide where you want to add the clip art.

2 Go to the **Insert** tab.

3 In the Illustrations group, click **Clip Art**, as Figure 7.12 shows.

4 Select your clip art from the Clip Art pane on the right side of your screen. More choices are available through the **Clip Art On Office Online** link at the bottom of the pane.

5 Click the selected piece of art.

When you open Clip Organizer for the first time, it's a good idea to let it scan your computer for photos and other media files. Clip

Figure 7.12
The Insert Clip Art command

Organizer will organise the files it finds into separate collections by leaving the files in their original locations and creating shortcuts to them. This lets you preview, open and insert files without digging through to their installed locations.

Follow these steps to allow Clip Organizer to scan automatically for clips:

1 In the Clip Art pane, click the **Organize Clips** link at the bottom of the pane.

2 In the Favorites – Microsoft Clip Organizer dialogue box, click **File**.

3 Click **Add Clips To Organizer**.

4 Click **Automatically**.

5 In the Add Clips To Organizer dialogue box, click **Options**. The process will take a few minutes.

6 In the Auto Import Settings dialogue box, select or clear the checkboxes for the folders you want the clips to be organised into.

7 Click **Catalog**.

8 Click **OK**.

→ Using SmartArt

When you use SmartArt, you can turn ho-hum graphics into wow! graphics. You can create, edit and animate SmartArt graphics, and paste them into Microsoft Office Excel 2007 and Microsoft Office Word 2007. You can also reuse SmartArt graphics from those programs.

There are seven types of graphic available for SmartArt: List, Process, Cycle, Hierarchy, Relationship, Matrix and Pyramid. Each offers a variety of layout options, as Table 7.1 shows.

Table 7.1

Graphic layout options available for SmartArt

To Do This	Choose this Layout
Show a continual process	Cycle
Show a decision tree or create an organisation chart	Hierarchy
Show non-sequential information	List
Show how parts relate to a whole	Matrix
Show process or timeline steps	Process
Show proportional relationships (largest component on top or bottom)	Pyramid
Illustrate connections	Relationship

7

Important

Some SmartArt layouts contain a fixed number of shapes, although most can be expanded. If you discover you are using a layout that is limited, you'll need to select a new layout to work with in order to add more shapes to it.

To create a SmartArt graphic, follow these steps:

1 Go to the **Insert** tab.

2 Click SmartArt in the Illustrations group, as shown in Figure 7.13.

3 In the left task pane of the Choose A SmartArt Graphic dialogue box, choose a layout type. The default is All, as in Figure 7.14.

Figure 7.13
The Insert SmartArt command

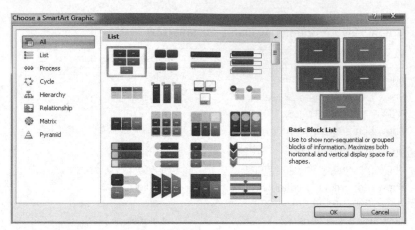

Figure 7.14
SmartArt layout options

4 Click a layout option. The task pane on the right offers a detailed description of the layout option you have selected.

5 Click **OK**.

6 Enter text as desired by typing it in the Type Your Text Here box or directly in the graphic.

7 Once you have entered your content, click the slide anywhere outside the graphic.

You can add or change text in a SmartArt graphic very easily by following these steps:

1 Click the SmartArt graphic.

2 In the Text pane that appears next to it, type in the text changes, as shown in Figure 7.15.

If you need to create a new line of bulleted text inside the Text pane, press **Enter** and then type the information on the new line. To indent a line inside the Text pane, select the line and click **Demote** in the Create Graphic group of the Design tab under SmartArt Tools.

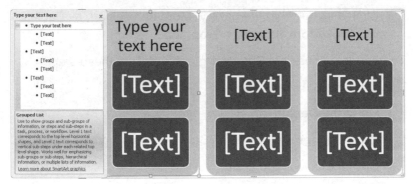

Figure 7.15
Text can be entered directly into a SmartArt graphic or by using the
Text pane, shown here on the left

7

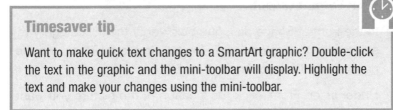

Timesaver tip

Want to make quick text changes to a SmartArt graphic? Double-click
the text in the graphic and the mini-toolbar will display. Highlight the
text and make your changes using the mini-toolbar.

You can also convert bulleted text to a SmartArt graphic very
easily. This can add a stronger visual impact to your slide. To
convert bulleted text into a SmartArt graphic, follow these steps:

1 Click the bulleted text placeholder.

2 Go to the **Home** tab.

3 Click **Convert to SmartArt** in the Paragraph group, as
Figure 7.16 shows.

Figure 7.16
The Convert to SmartArt command

4 Click a layout from the gallery. More choices are available if you click **More SmartArt Graphics**.

To change colours in a SmartArt graphic, follow these steps:

1 Click the SmartArt graphic.

2 Go to the **Design** tab.

3 Click **Change Colors** in the SmartArt Styles group.

4 Click the colour you prefer.

You can add a picture as a background to a SmartArt graphic, too. To do that, follow these steps:

1 Right-click the SmartArt graphic border.

2 Click **Format Object**.

3 In the Format Shape dialogue box, verify the Fill category is selected in the task pane on the left. In the task pane on the right, select **Picture Or Texture Fill**.

4 Under Insert From, click the location of the picture you want to insert (File, Clipboard or ClipArt).

5 If you want the picture to be transparent, tiled, stretched, offset or rotated, make your choices now. Select **Rotate with Shape** to avoid frustrations if you play around with the graphic later.

6 Click **Close**.

Although SmartArt graphics are designed to be used as is, there may be occasions when you want to modify a graphic by adding a shape to it. To add a shape to your graphic, follow these steps:

1 Select your graphic.

2 Select a shape within the graphic next to where you want the new shape to go.

3 Under SmartArt Tools, on the Design tab, go to the **Create Graphic** group.

4 Click **Add Shape**.

5 Choose the new shape's placement by selecting **Add Shape After**, **Before**, **Above** or **Below**. The shape will be placed in reference to the shape you have selected within the graphic.

→ Adding Charts

Charts can help your audience focus on key points quickly and easily. With the QuickStyle Gallery offered in PowerPoint 2007, you can find the chart style you want with minimal effort. In fact, the Insert Chart dialogue box shows you all chart options for a given chart type. Charts can be embedded or inserted into your presentation, and you can paste or link to Excel 2007 charts. When you embed an Excel 2007 chart, you can edit the data in Excel 2007, but the worksheet saves with your PowerPoint 2007 file. If you copy or link to the chart, you must make changes to the actual worksheet – it is still a separate file and will not save with your PowerPoint 2007 file.

There are 11 main chart types to choose from:

- **Column** – arranges data into columns with categories organised along the horizontal axis and values along the vertical axis.

- **Line** – plots data into lines on a chart with categories organised on the horizontal axis and values along the vertical axis.

- **Pie** – arranges data as a percentage of an entire pie.

- **Bar** – uses bars to illustrate differences in individual pieces of data.

- **Area** – draws attention to trends by arranging data into horizontal areas that show relationships of each part to the whole.

- **XY** – arranges data in a scattered format on a chart.

- **Stock** – arranges data in a specific order to illustrate fluctuations in stock prices. Can also be used for scientific data.

- **Surface** – shows the optimum combinations between two sets of numerical data.

- **Doughnut** – similar to a pie chart, but can contain more than one data series.

- **Bubble** – similar to XY charts, but can compare sets of three instead of two values.

- **Radar** – compares aggregate values of a number of data series.

To create a chart in PowerPoint 2007, follow these steps:

1 In Normal view, select the slide where you want to place the chart.

2 Go to the **Insert** tab, and click **Chart** in the Illustrations group.

3 In the Insert Chart dialogue box, click the chart type you want, as shown in Figure 7.17. Click **OK**.

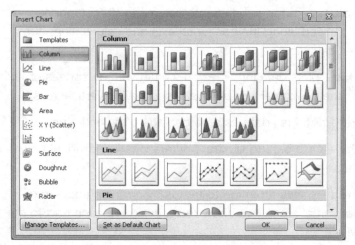

Figure 7.17
Chart options

4 The chart will be placed on your slide, and Excel 2007 will open a corresponding worksheet.

> ## Important
>
> When you use a diagram that was originally created in Excel, Word or PowerPoint 2003, you can convert the diagram to an updated graphic for PowerPoint 2007. Just double-click the diagram and then select whether you want to convert it to a SmartArt graphic or a shape.

Saving a Chart Template

You can easily save and reuse a chart that you have created by saving it as a chart template. To save a chart as a chart template, follow these steps:

1 Click the chart you want to save as the template.

2 Go to the **Design** tab.

3 Under Chart Tools, click **Save As Template** in the Type group.

4 Select the **Charts** folder in the Save In box of the Save Chart Template window.

5 In the File Name box, type the appropriate name for the chart.

6 Click **Save**.

To reuse the chart, select the **Templates** folder in the Insert Chart dialogue box, and then click your template to retrieve your chart.

Formatting Chart Elements

You can apply formatting to individual chart elements such as data markers, the chart area, the plot area and the numbers and text in titles and labels. You can either apply specific shape styles and WordArt styles or format the shapes and text of chart elements manually.

To format chart elements, follow these steps:

1 Click to select the chart element you want to format.

2 Click the **Format** tab under Chart Tools.

3 In the Current Selection group, click the **Chart Elements** arrow.

- The names of a series, plot area, legend or axis will be displayed. Hover the cursor on the arrow in the box at the top of the Current Selection group, and the Chart Elements label text should appear, as in Figure 7.18.

4 Select the chart element you want to format.

5 Do one or more of the following:

- Click **Format Selection** and make changes as desired in the Format chart element dialogue box. Click **Close**.

- In the Shape Styles group on the Format tab under Chart Tools, make any desired changes to Visual Style, Shape Fill, Shape Outline or Shape Effects for the chart.

- In the WordArt Styles group, make any desired changes to Text Style, Text Fill, Text Outline or Text Effects.

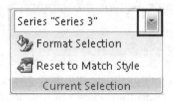

Figure 7.18
The Chart Elements command

8

Adding Columns, Tables and Lists

In this chapter, you will learn how to work with columns and tables and how to use lists to your advantage.

→ Working with Columns

When you work with text in a presentation, there might be times when you want to place the text into columns. For example, if you want to create a presentation that looks like a newspaper layout, you may need the text to flow into a column format. You don't need to create a table to do this if you don't want to (although using a table can accomplish the same effect in some ways).

Instead, you need to turn the text box into a text box with columns. To do this, follow these steps:

1 Click the text box.

2 Right-click the border.

3 In the shortcut menu, click **Format Shape**.

4 In the Format Shape dialogue box, click **Text Box** in the left pane.

5 In the right pane, click **Columns**, as in Figure 8.1.

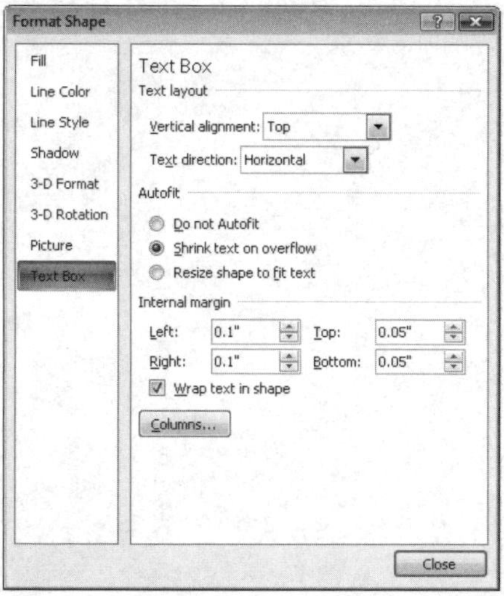

Figure 8.1
The Columns command

6 Specify the number of columns you want and the spacing that should be between them, as Figure 8.2 shows.

7 Click **OK**.

8 Click **Close**.

The text in the text box will now flow automatically into both columns, just like it does in a traditional newspaper column format.

Figure 8.2
The Columns dialogue box

→ Working with Tables

Tables are a great way to compile information and display it in an easy-to-understand format. You can instantly add a new table to your presentation with automatic tables, or you can draw your own tables. Updating throughout the Office 2007 system makes sharing tables between Word, Excel and PowerPoint a pretty simple process.

Before you create any tables, however, it's important to think about the audience who will be viewing the presentation. If you will routinely be passing the presentation to people who do not have PowerPoint 2007, you need to know that there are some table compatibility issues between PowerPoint 2007 and earlier versions of PowerPoint.

Specifically, the new features of PowerPoint 2007 listed in Table 8.1 should be avoided if the presentation is to be used in earlier versions. If you do use an action that should be avoided,

PowerPoint 2007 will convert your table to a picture in earlier versions of PowerPoint.

Table 8.1
Caption to come?

Action to Avoid	Action to Use Instead
Using all QuickStyles under Best Match for Document	Only use No Style, Table Grid or No Style, No Grid
Using background fills as a shape or applying a QuickStyle with a background shape	Only use No Style, Table Grid or No Style, No Grid, or use a QuickStyle under Light, Medium and Dark
Using visual effects (shadows, bevels, etc.) or applying pictures, gradients and texture fills to cells or text	Do not use effects
Using WordArt to create text in table cells	Do not use WordArt for table text
Changing text orientation	Do not change text orientation

Adding a Table

You can easily add a table to your presentation with the standard options provided by PowerPoint. Follow these steps:

1 Go to the **Insert** tab.

2 Click **Table** in the Table group.

3 In the Insert Table box, select the number of rows and columns for your table by pulling your cursor across the rows and columns of cells until you have the correct number of each for your table. Your slide will show the table as you select or deselect cells, as in Figure 8.3.

4 Click the final box in the table to add the table to your slide.

To add a row to a table, follow these steps:

1 Click a cell in the row above or below where you want the new row to appear.

2 Go to the **Layout** tab under Table Tools.

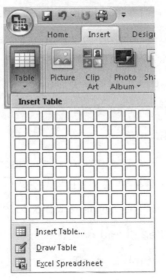

Figure 8.3
The Insert Table command

3 In the Table group, click **Select**.

4 Click **Select Row**.

5 In the Rows & Columns group, click **Insert Above** or **Insert Below**, depending upon your needs, as shown in Figure 8.4.

Timesaver tip

You can quickly add a row to the bottom of your table by clicking the last cell in the last row and then pressing **Tab** on your keyboard.

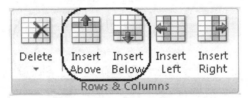

Figure 8.4
Adding rows to a chart

To add a column to a table, follow these steps:

1 Click a cell in the column to the right or left of where you want the new column to appear.

2 Go to the **Layout** tab under Table Tools.

3 In the Table group, click **Select**.

4 Click **Select Column**.

5 In the Rows & Columns group, click **Insert Left** or **Insert Right**, depending upon your needs, as Figure 8.5 shows.

To delete a column or row within a table, follow these steps:

1 Click a cell in the column or row that you want to delete.

2 Go to the **Layout** tab under Table Tools.

3 In the Table group, click **Select**.

4 Click **Select Column** or **Select Row**.

5 In the Rows & Columns group, click **Delete**.

6 Click **Delete Rows** or **Delete Columns**, depending on your needs, as in Figure 8.6.

To merge cells within a table, follow these steps:

1 Highlight the cells you want to merge. They must be next to each other in some way.

2 Go to the **Layout** tab under Table Tools.

3 In the Merge group, click **Merge Cells**, as Figure 8.7 shows.

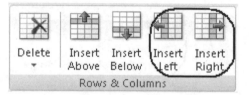

Figure 8.5
Adding columns to a chart

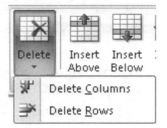

Figure 8.6
The Delete Columns command

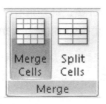

Figure 8.7
The Merge Cells command

If you need to split cells, follow the steps above and, in step 3, click **Split Cells** instead of Merge Cells.

Understanding and Applying Table Styles

Now that you have a table in your presentation, let's take a few minutes to explore table styles. When you add a table to a presentation, a style is applied to it automatically, based on the overall presentation theme you have chosen. Change the theme, and the look of your table will change as well. If you don't want a table to reflect the overall presentation theme, you need to apply a table style.

Table Styles are formatting options that you can select to change the look and feel of your table. Although you always have the option of changing a single cell or combination of cells, using Table Styles allows you to apply preset formatting combinations. Specifically:

■ Each style is shown in a thumbnail view in the Table Styles group.

- Styles can be added or changed by double-clicking the table and making a selection from the Table Styles or QuickStyles group.

- Previews of how the style will impact your table can be seen simply by holding the cursor over the style.

- Styles can be removed by selecting **Clear Table** from the Table Styles group More button.

- QuickStyle options include banded rows and columns, special formatting for the first and last columns in a table, turning the Total row on and off, and turning on and off special formatting for the header row.

To apply a Table Style to a table, follow these steps:

1 Click the table.

2 Go to the **Design** tab under Table Tools, shown in Figure 8.8.

Important

You're not seeing double if you see two Design tabs in your Ribbon. This can happen when you have selected a table – the Table Tools tab will appear with a Design tab that is separate from the original design tab on the Ribbon. Table Tools Design holds commands specifically for table formatting; the other Design tab holds commands that can be applied to all other aspects of your presentation.

3 Click the **More** arrow ▾ in the Table Styles group.

4 Click the Table Style you prefer.

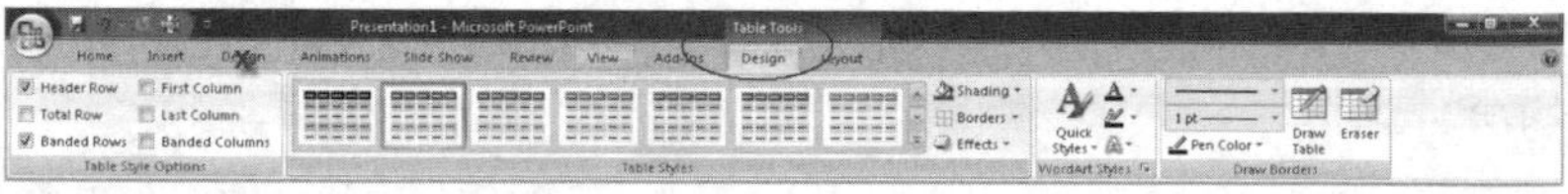

Figure 8.8
Table Tools Design tab

Drawing a Table

If you prefer simply to draw your own table instead, follow these steps:

1 Go to the **Insert** tab.

2 Click **Table** in the Table group.

3 Click **Draw Table**. Notice that your cursor changes to a pencil.

4 Using the "pencil", define the boundaries of your table by dragging the cursor first diagonally to the size that you want, and then dragging it within the table to make row and column boundaries, as in Figure 8.9.

5 When you have drawn the table to your satisfaction, enter text into your cells.

Figure 8.9
Drawing a table

Timesaver tip

Need to erase a line in the table you've drawn? Use the **Eraser** command in the Draw Borders group on the Table Tools Design tab.

Copying a Table from Word or Excel

You can easily reuse tables that have already been created in Word 2007 or Excel 2007 by copying them into your PowerPoint presentation. Then, once you have inserted a table into your presentation, use the Table Tools Design tab to make any changes to design and style. Follow these steps:

1 In Word or Excel, select the table you want to copy.

2 In Word or Excel, go to the **Clipboard** group on the Home tab and click **Copy**.

3 In PowerPoint, select the slide you want to copy the table to.

4 In PowerPoint, go to the **Clipboard** group on the Home tab and click **Paste**.

> **Important**
>
> Text within a table will not appear on the Outline tab of your presentation. Only text from placeholders appears in that tab.

Inserting a Table Directly from Excel

When you insert a table directly from Excel, you can use the actual functionality of Excel in your presentation. The table becomes an embedded object, however, so you cannot make changes to the table to match your PowerPoint theme. Also, you cannot edit the table with PowerPoint options.

1 In PowerPoint, select the slide where you want to place the table.

2 Go to the **Insert** tab and click **Table** in the Table group.

3 Click **Insert Excel Table**. When the Excel table appears on the slide, add text by clicking a cell and entering the text.

Changing Colours in a Table

To change background colours in a table, follow these steps:

1 Click the table.

2 Go to the **Table Tools Design** tab.

3 Click **Shading** in the Table Styles group, as Figure 8.10 shows.

4 Click the colour you prefer.

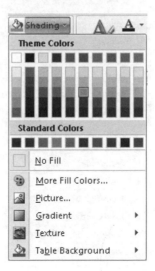

Figure 8.10
Shading commands

Jargon buster

Grid lines These are the lines that appear in a table as a table border and as internal cell borders.

Working with Grid Lines

To change the background colours in a table, follow these steps:

1 Click the table.

2 Go to the **Table Tools Design** tab.

3 Click the **Borders** button ⊞ Borders ▾ in the Table Styles group. Note: this button will change names, depending upon the grid lines already applied to the table.

4 Click the border option you prefer, as in Figure 8.11. You might need to click multiple options to achieve the look you want.

Figure 8.11
Border options

→ Working with Lists

Lists are a great way to prioritise content and make it easy for viewers to read and understand. In PowerPoint, you can have bulleted lists, numbered lists and multilevel lists. Don't go crazy with lists, however. Readers can quickly become overwhelmed if, for example, every page in your presentation has a list, or the list is so crammed with information that it's difficult to read quickly. Keep lists to a minimum on your page and, if you must include a lot of information in a bullet, consider using a multilevel list to help break up the text for readers.

To add a bulleted list to your presentation, follow these steps:

1 Highlight the text you want to bullet.

2 Go to the **Home** tab.

3 Click **Bullets** in the Paragraph group.

If you don't like the style that was applied, click the down arrow next to Bullets to see the options, as shown in Figure 8.12.

This displays a full list of bullet options and even provides you with options for creating your own bullets. Select a new style from the menu provided, or click **Bullets and Numbering** and then follow these steps:

1 In the Bullets and Numbering dialogue box, click **Customize**.

2 In the Font box, select the font you want to use.

3 Click a symbol from the options shown, using the scroll bar to see all your options, as in Figure 8.13.

4 Click **OK**.

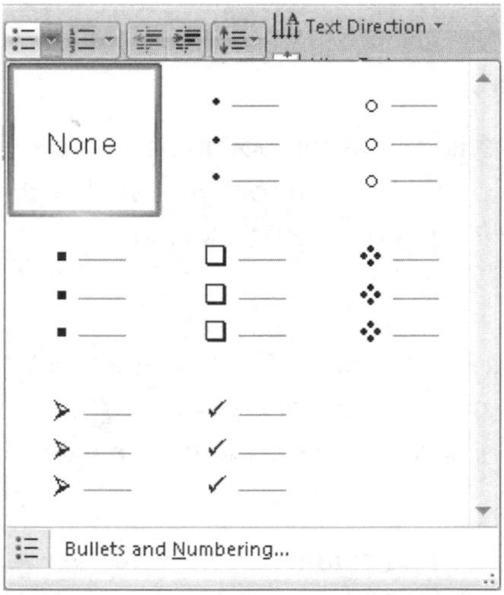

Figure 8.12
Bullet options

Figure 8.13
There are numerous ways to customize bullets

Instead of clicking **Customize** in the steps above, you can also elect to choose a picture for your bullet. To do that, follow these steps:

1. Highlight the text you want to bullet.

2. Go to the **Home** tab.

3. Click the down arrow next to Bullets in the Paragraph group.

4. Click **Bullets and Numbering**.

5. Click **Picture**.

6. Make a selection from the options provided, or click **Import** to import a particular picture. If you click **Import**, locate and select the picture and then click **Add**.

7. Click **OK**.

The steps for adding numbered lists flow almost identically to bulleted lists, except that instead of clicking the **Bullets** command you click the **Numbering** command in the Paragraph group.

Multilevel lists aren't an actual option within PowerPoint like they are with some Office 2007 programs, but you can easily create them using the **Increase List Level** or **Decrease List Level** options in the Paragraph group of the Home tab. These commands indent or remove indents from a list line.

To create a multilevel list, follow these steps:

1 In a bulleted or numbered list, place the cursor in the line you want to indent.

2 Go to the **Paragraph** tab.

3 Click **Increase List Level**. If you want to decrease the line instead, click **Decrease List Level**.

8

Timesaver tip

You can adjust indenting on all bulleted and numbered lists in your presentation by using the Slide Master instead of a single slide.

9

Adding Animation to Your Presentation

In this chapter, you will learn how to work with media clips, slide animation and slide transitions. You will learn to add sound and video to your presentations and how to make inanimate objects move on the screen.

→ Working with Sound

Many people tend to forget that PowerPoint can use sound in conjunction with words and pictures. When used appropriately, sound can add impact and a little fun to a presentation. As you explore using sound in your presentation, keep in mind that it needs to emphasise a key point – if it doesn't, then it shouldn't be used.

In PowerPoint 2007, you can embed Windows Audio (.*wav*) files smaller than 100 kilobytes (kB) in a presentation. Any other media file types must be linked to the presentation.

As well as .*wav* files, there are five other compatible sound file formats that can be used with PowerPoint 2007, as shown in Table 9.1.

Table 9.1

Compatible Sound File formats

Compatible Sound Formats	Standard File Format Extension
Audio Interchange File Format	.aiff
AU Audio file	.au
Musical Instrument Digital Interface	.midi
MPEG Audio Layer 3	.mp3
Windows Media Audio file	.wma

Adding Basic Sound

To add sound to your presentation, follow these steps:

1 Select the slide where the sound will be placed.

2 Go to the **Insert** tab.

3 Click the arrow on the Sound button in the Media Clips group. Note: clicking the arrow on the Sound button will provide you with a menu of options, as in Figure 9.1. If you click the icon *above* Sound, the Insert Sound dialogue box appears.

4 Select from the following options: **Sound from File**, **Sound from Clip Organizer, Play CD Audio Track** and **Record Sound**. For the purposes of this example, click **Sound From Clip Organizer**.

5 In the Clip Art task pane, double-click the sound you want to add.

6 Click **Automatically** in the Microsoft Office PowerPoint dialogue box, as Figure 9.2 shows.

7 Test your sound by clicking the **Slide Show** button next to the Zoom slider at the bottom right of your screen, as in Figure 9.3.

Figure 9.1
The Sound menu

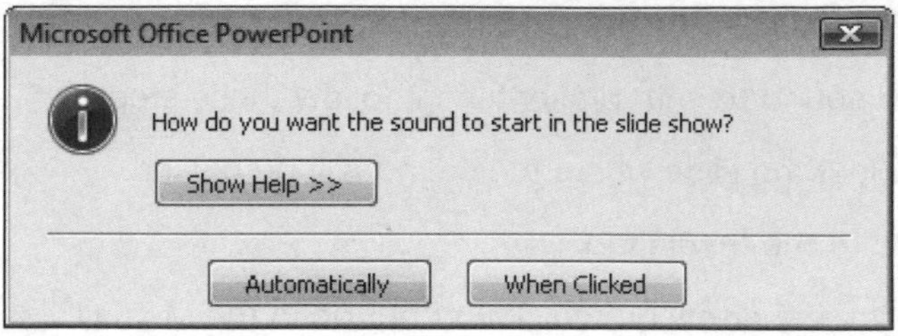

![Microsoft Office PowerPoint dialog: How do you want the sound to start in the slide show? Show Help >> Automatically | When Clicked]

Figure 9.2
You can play sound automatically

Figure 9.3
Test sound using the slides

Timesaver tip

You can also preview sounds by double-clicking the sound icon on the slide. Or, go to the **Sound Tools Options** tab and click **Preview** in the Play group.

Modifying Stop and Start Settings

When you use sound in PowerPoint, it will play once by default. However, you can change the default so that sound keeps playing throughout the rest of the presentation or until it is stopped purposely. To change the default so that the sound starts differently, follow these steps:

1. Click the sound icon on the slide.

2. Go to the **Animations** tab.

3. Click **Custom Animation** in the Animations group, as shown in Figure 9.4.

4. In the Custom Animation task pane, click the down arrow in the Start box, as Figure 9.5 shows.

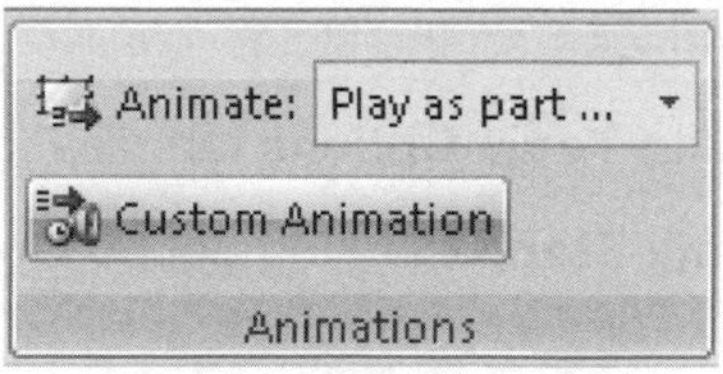

Figure 9.4
The Custom Animation command

Figure 9.5
The Custom Animation task pane

5 Select when you want the sound to start (**On Click**, **With Previous** or **After Previous**), as shown in Figure 9.6.

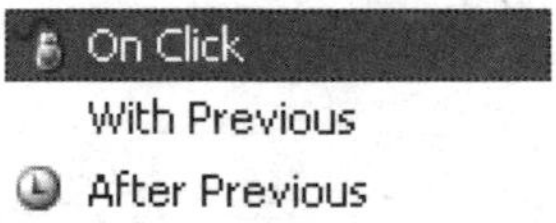

Figure 9.6
Sounds start at your command

To change the default so that the sound repeats continuously, follow these steps:

1 Click the sound icon on the slide.

2 Go to the **Sound Tools Options** tab, as Figure 9.7 shows.

3 Click **Loop Until Stopped** in the Sound Options groups, as in Figure 9.8.

To modify settings that tell the sound when to stop, follow these steps:

1 Click the sound icon on the slide.

2 Go to the **Animations** tab.

3 Click **Custom Animation** in the Animations group.

4 In the Custom Animation task pane, click the down arrow to the right of the sound, as shown in Figure 9.9.

5 In the shortcut menu, click **Effect Options**.

6 In the Play Sound dialogue box, click the **Effect** tab.

7 Select from the following options under Stop playing, as shown in Figure 9.10:

- **On click**

- **After current slide**

- **After X slides** (insert the relevant number).

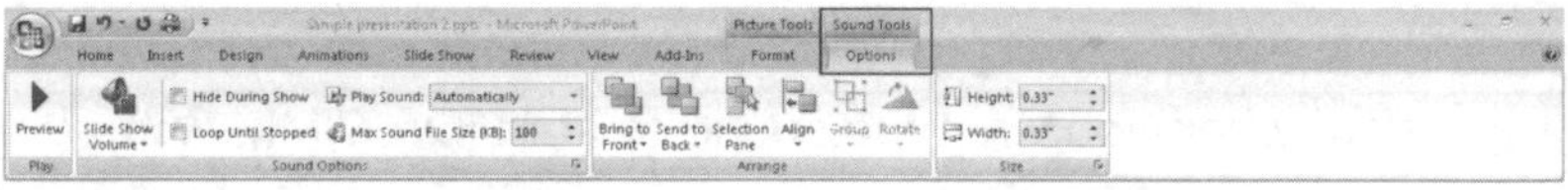

Figure 9.7
The Sound Tools Options tab

Figure 9.8
You can loop sound in PowerPoint 2007

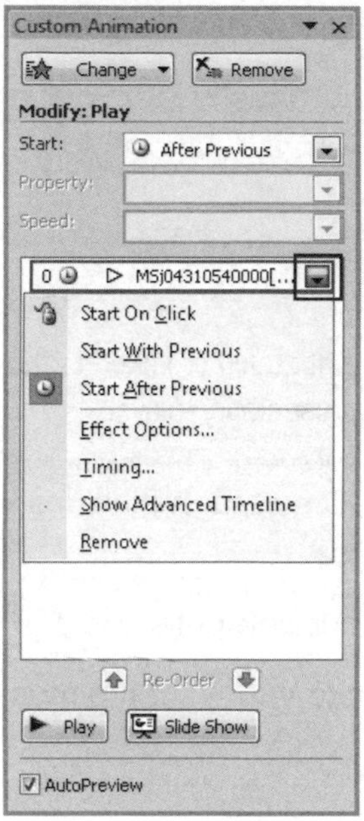

Figure 9.9
The arrow to the right of the command

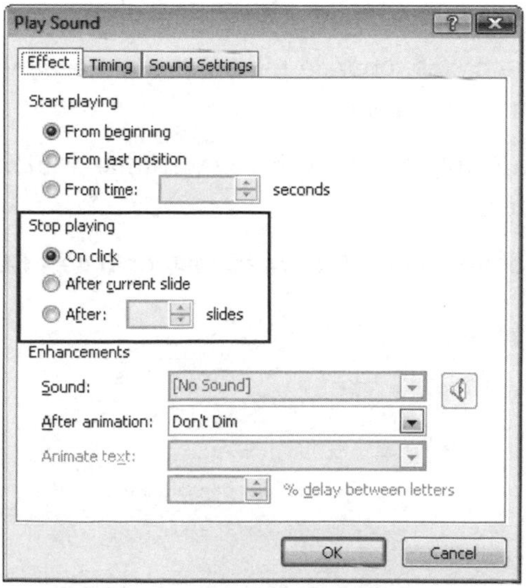

Figure 9.10
Stop playing options

Playing a CD During a Presentation

Instead of adding sound directly into your presentation, you can use music from a CD with it.

> **Important**
>
> Music from a CD is not embedded or linked to the presentation. It plays separately as the presentation plays.

To add audio from a CD so that it plays as your presentation runs, follow these steps:

1 Insert the CD in your computer's CD drive.

2 Click the slide where you want the music to begin playing.

3 Go to the **Insert** tab.

4 Click the arrow under Sound in the Media Clips group.

5 Click **Play CD Audio Track**, as in Figure 9.11.

6 In the Insert CD Audio dialogue box, enter the starting and ending track numbers, as Figure 9.12 shows.

7 In the time boxes, change the times if necessary; otherwise, these can be left alone.

8 Click **Loop Until Stopped** if you want the audio to play continuously.

9 At the prompt, select **Automatically** or **When Clicked**.

Figure 9.11
The Play CD Audio Track command

Insert CD Audio

Clip selection

Start at track: 1   time: 00:00   seconds

End at track: 14   time: 02:57.12   seconds

Play options

☐ Loop until stopped

Sound volume: 🔊

Display options

☐ Hide sound icon during slide show

Information

Total playing time: 1:07:08.95
File: [CD Audio]

OK   Cancel

Figure 9.12
The Insert CD Audio dialogue box

9

Timesaver tip

If you want to play music from different tracks from a CD during different slides, just set the timing as needed under Clip Selection in the Insert CD Audio dialogue box when performing the steps for Playing a CD During a Presentation.

Package for CD

When you use sound, PowerPoint 2007 creates a link to a sound or movie file's current location on your computer. If that sound or movie file is moved, PowerPoint 2007 can't find it. It's critical that when a presentation is e-mailed or used on another computer, the linked files are copied along with the PowerPoint 2007 file into the same folder.

The best way to do this is to use the Package for CD feature. This copies your files to a single location on a CD or in a folder and automatically updates sound and movie file links. To use the Package for CD feature, follow these steps:

1 Click the **Microsoft Office** button.

2 Click **Publish**.

3 Click **Package for CD**, as Figure 9.13 shows.

4 In the Package for CD dialogue box, type in the name for the CD, as shown in Figure 9.14.

5 Click **Copy to CD**. Note: don't forget to put a CD in your drive before this step!

6 Click **Yes** when asked whether you want to include linked files in the package.

7 After the CD is copied, click **Close**.

There are more options available with this process. For example, you can specify in which order multiple presentations should play or whether you want a password applied before the presentation can be opened. To see all the options available and to make any selections, click **Options** in the Package for CD dialogue box before you click **Copy to CD**.

Figure 9.13
The Package for CD command

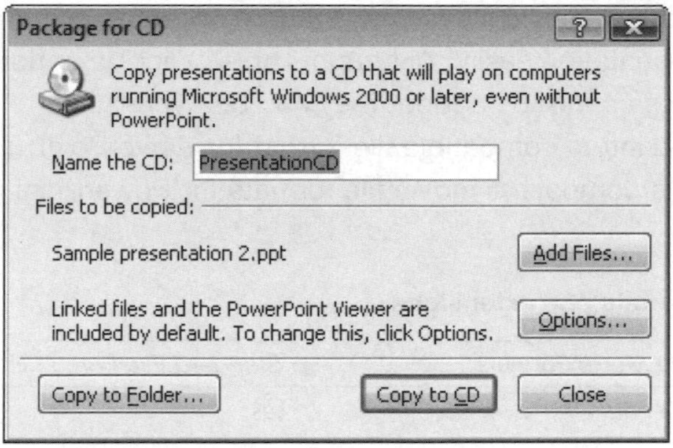

Figure 9.14
The Package for CD dialogue box

→ Working with Media Clips

Adding movies to a presentation can be a fun way to break up an abundance of text and add a professional element to your presentation. Movies are often used for demonstrations, but they can also be used for training purposes.

Movie files cannot be embedded in a presentation; instead, you must create a link so that PowerPoint can easily find and use the movie file. As a result, you must always store movie files on the same computer that will be used to play the presentation. When they play, they can show on just part of a slide or in full-screen mode. Full-screen mode, however, sometimes produces blurs or distortion, depending upon the resolution of the movie clip, so be careful when using this option.

Important

Animated GIF files are sometimes referred to as movies, but really they aren't movie files. If you use a *.gif* file as a movie in your presentation, you won't be able to use all movie options, since it is technically not a movie file.

Four standard movie file formats can be added to a PowerPoint 2007 presentation easily. Although Apple QuickTime movies (*.mov*) files cannot be added, they can be hyperlinked to or converted into a compatible file format for PowerPoint. Table 9.2 shows the compatible movie file formats for PowerPoint 2007.

Table 9.2
Movie formats and extensions

Compatible Movie Formats	*Standard File Format Extension*
Windows Media File	*.asf*
Windows Video File	*.avi*
Movie File	*.mpg or .mpeg*
Windows Media Video File	*.wmv*

To add a movie to your presentation, follow these steps:

1 Select the slide where the movie will be added.

2 Go to the **Insert** tab.

3 In the Media Clips group, click the arrow on the Movie button.

4 Click **Movie from File** or **Movie from Clip Organizer**, depending upon where the movie file is located, as shown in Figure 9.15.

5 Locate and select the movie to place it on the slide.

6 At the prompt, click **Automatically** or **When Clicked**. (*.gif* files will not show this option.)

Figure 9.15
Movie commands

Timesaver tip

To prevent movies from skipping during playback, go to the **Movie Tools Options** tab and click the **More** arrow in the Size group. Place a checkmark in Best Scale for Slide Show.

To show the movie in full-screen mode, follow these steps:

1. Click the movie frame on the slide.
2. Go to the **Movie Tools Options** tab.
3. Place a checkmark next to Play Full Screen in the Movie Options group, as shown in Figure 9.16.
4. To preview the movie to check for distortion or blurriness, click **Preview** in the Play group under Movie Tools Options.

You can resize a movie by clicking and dragging its borders to the size you want. The centre of the movie will remain in place if you press **CTRL** while dragging the borders.

Timesaver tip

If you choose the option to start the movie automatically, you can drag the movie frame off the slide completely so that your audience never sees the movie frame at all.

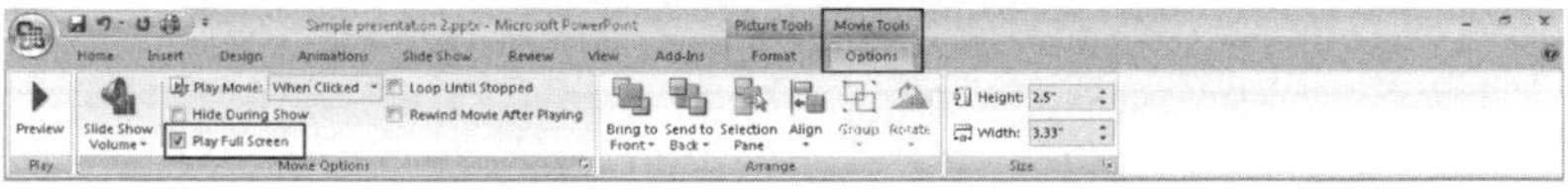

Figure 9.16
The Movie Tools Options tab

→ Adding Slide Animation

You can add custom animation to almost any item on a slide, including placeholders, paragraphs, single bullets and list items. There are probably hundreds of ways to animate an object, but it's a good idea to keep animation to a minimum in order to avoid distracting your audience.

When you work with animations, you will be using the Custom Animation pane to control how the item appears on the slide and to control the order of multiple effects in relation to one another.

To display the Custom Animation pane, follow these steps:

1 Click the slide where the animation will appear.

2 Go to the **Animations** tab.

3 Click **Custom Animation** in the Animations group, as Figure 9.17 shows.

The Custom Animation task pane will appear on the right side of your screen. However, until you select an object for animation, the options in the pane will be unavailable. Go ahead and place an item on the slide that you can use to test animation.

Now, take a moment to review the Initial Custom Animation task pane options available to you:

- Add Effect
- Remove

Figure 9.17
The Custom Animation command

- Start

- Path

- Speed

- Play

- Slide Show

- AutoPreview.

As you work with animations, notice that you can usually modify the start, direction and speed of the animation with each object. However, depending upon the effect chosen, your options might be limited or even expanded to include more options.

Creating a Simple Animation

To add simple animation to an object, follow these steps:

1 Click the object you want to animate.

2 Click **Add Effect** in the Custom Animation task pane.

3 Click when you want the effect to occur (**Entrance**, **Exit** or **Emphasis**), as shown in Figure 9.18.

4 Click the effect you want by selecting from the mini-menu or choosing **More Effects** to see additional options.

Creating a Simple Motion Path

To add a simple motion path animation to an object, follow these steps:

1 Click the object you want to animate.

2 Click **Add Effect** in the Custom Animation task pane.

3 Click **Motion Path**.

4 Click a motion path option from the menu, as shown in Figure 9.19.

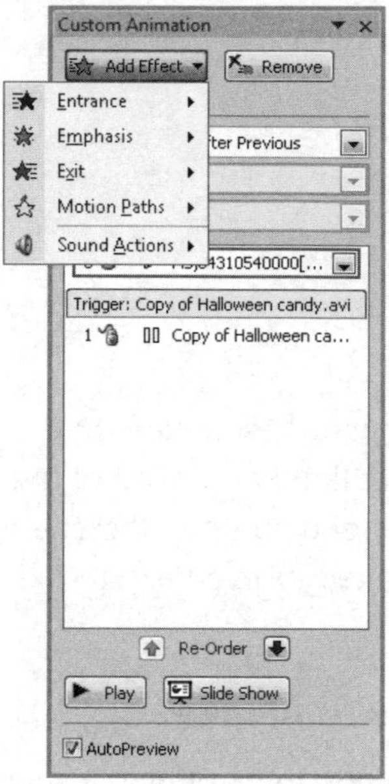

Figure 9.18
The Animation Commands menu

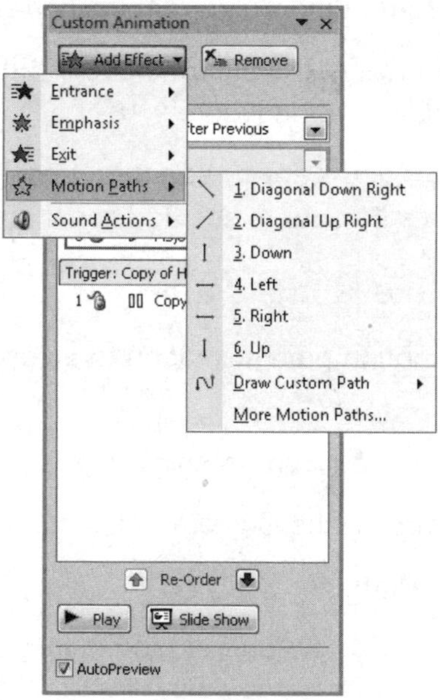

Figure 9.19
Motion Path options

Creating a Custom Animation Path

If you want your animation to be a bit more advanced, you can create a custom animation path so that the object moves anywhere on the slide that you designate.

To create a custom animation path, follow these steps:

1 Click the object you want to animate.

2 Click **Add Effect** in the Custom Animation task pane.

3 Click **Motion Path**.

4 Click **Draw Custom Path**.

5 Click one of these options: **Line**, **Curve**, **Freeform** or **Scribble**.

6 Using your cursor as a pencil, draw the animation path on the slide, as in Figure 9.20.

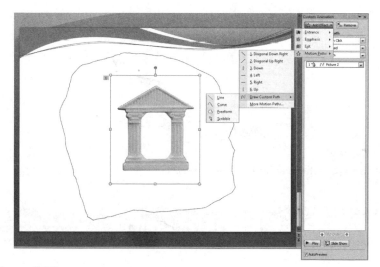

Figure 9.20
A sample Animation Path

Changing Animation Order

If you need to change the animation order, follow these steps:

1 Select the object in the Custom Animation task pane.

2 Drag the object to the new location in the task pane. You can also use the re-order arrows at the bottom of the task pane.

As you drag objects up or down, a solid line will appear. You can drop the item wherever a solid line is shown, as in Figure 9.21.

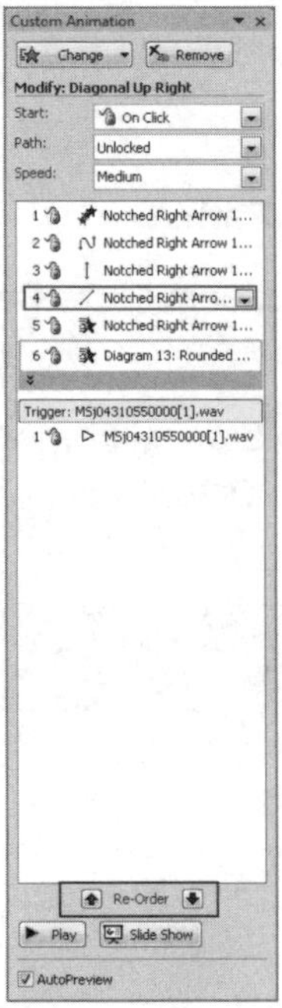

Figure 9.21
Drop items where solid lines are shown

→ Animating SmartArt Graphics

SmartArt graphics can be animated just like other objects. However, when you animate such a graphic, keep the following in mind:

■ Connecting lines between shapes do not animate individually. They are always associated with the second shape.

- Animation plays in the order that shapes within a SmartArt graphic appear. However, you can reverse the order for the entire object.

- Diagrams created in earlier versions of PowerPoint and converted to SmartArt graphics might lose some animation settings or appear differently.

SmartArt graphics can be animated in a range of ways, depending upon the layout involved. Take your time to experiment with different graphics to see how different levels and shapes react to different animation instructions.

To animate a SmartArt object, follow these steps:

1 Click the SmartArt graphic.

2 Go to the **Animations** tab.

3 In the Animations group, click the arrow to the right of Animate. There may be text in the box beside Animate that says "No Animation", or it might show other animation effect text, as Figure 9.22 shows.

4 Click an animation effect from the options provided in the menu.

Figure 9.22
SmartArt animation options

→ Using Slide Transitions

When you use slide transitions in a presentation, try to use them in a consistent way so that your audience doesn't become distracted. For example, if you start out using a particular transition format, continue it with the other slides in the presentation. Using different transitions for every slide can cause your audience to become more preoccupied with the transition than with the content the transition is leading to.

With transitions, you can make a slide fade away slowly or make it open quickly and with a lot of pizzazz. You can even add sound to a transition.

To apply the same slide transition to all slides, follow these steps:

1 In Normal view, click the **Slide** tab.

2 Click any slide thumbnail in the pane.

3 Go to the **Animations** tab.

4 Click a transition style from the QuickStyles Gallery in the Transition To This Slide group. Use the More arrow to see further options, as in Figure 9.23.

5 In the same group, click the arrow to the right of Transition Sound, and then click the sound you want to use (if any), as Figure 9.24 shows.

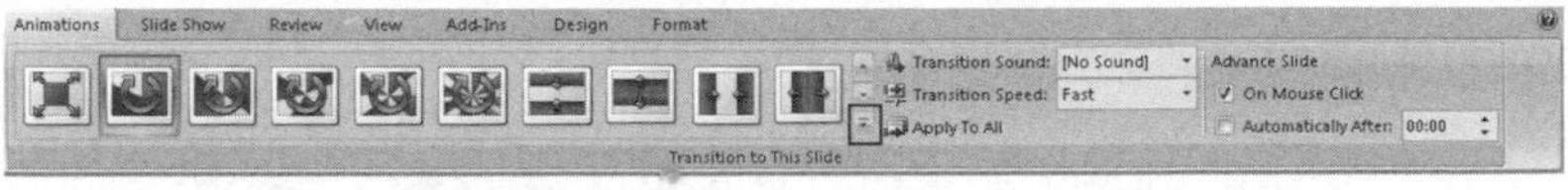

Figure 9.23
The More arrow

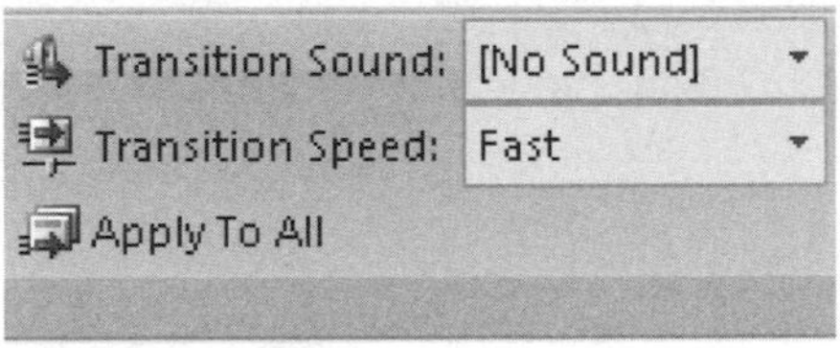

Figure 9.24
The Transition Sound command

9

6 In the same group, click the arrow to the right of Transition Speed, and then click the appropriate speed (Slow, Medium or Fast).

7 In the same group, click **Apply To All**.

To add a different slide transition to each slide, follow these steps:

1 In Normal view, click the **Slide** tab.

2 Click the slide thumbnail where you want the transition applied.

3 Go to the **Animations** tab, and click a transition style in the QuickStyles Gallery of the Transition To This Slide group.

4 In the same group, click the arrow to the right of Transition Sound, and then click the sound you want to use.

5 In the same group, click the arrow to the right of Transition Speed, and then click the appropriate speed.

6 To make additional transitions for other slides, repeat steps 1–5.

10

Working with PowerPoint Objects

In this chapter, you will learn how to work with PowerPoint objects by using rotating and resizing tools, grouping and ungrouping objects, and cutting, copying and pasting objects. You'll also learn how to select and move objects.

→ Selecting an Object

As you work with objects, you will need to select multiple objects in order to group them together. There are several ways to do this. To select a few objects on a slide, follow these steps:

1 Click the first object.

2 Press the **Shift** key on your keyboard.

3 While holding down the **Shift** key, click the additional objects you want to group together, as shown in Figure 10.1.

Timesaver tip

You can select all objects on a slide by going to the **Home** tab and clicking **Select** in the Editing group. Then just click **Select All**.

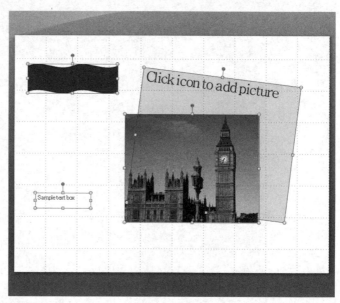

Figure 10.1
When you select multiple objects, each object will show resizing and rotating handles.

To select hidden, layered or stacked objects, follow these steps:

1 Go to the **Home** tab.

2 Click **Select** in the Editing group.

3 Click **Select Objects**.

4 Using your cursor, draw a box around the hidden or stacked objects, as shown in Figure 10.2. Note: you must draw from the outside of all objects that you are selecting; if you start from within any of the objects, that object will not be selected.

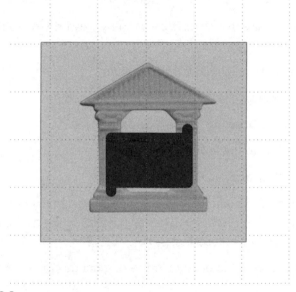

Figure 10.2
A box around hidden/stacked objects

→ Using Layered Objects

You can group a variety of objects together, including pictures, charts, graphs and text. When you group things together, the result is a "layered object". Layered objects can be flipped, rotated, moved and resized at the same time as a single object.

Grouping and Ungrouping Objects

Grouping objects allows you to work more quickly in some cases, since you don't have to take multiple actions in order to accomplish the same task for multiple objects.

To group objects together, follow these steps:

 Select the objects you want to group.

2 Go to the **Drawing Tools Format** tab.

3 Click **Group** in the Arrange group.

4 Click **Group**, as shown in Figure 10.3.

The multiple objects will now be seen by PowerPoint as a single object.

To ungroup objects, follow these steps:

1 Select the layered object to be ungrouped.

2 Go to the **Drawing Tools Format** tab.

3 Click **Group** in the Arrange group.

4 Click **Ungroup**, as Figure 10.4 shows.

Sometimes, when you work with a group, you may ungroup it and then need to regroup it. Rather than selecting all the objects again, follow these steps instead:

 Select one of the objects in the original group.

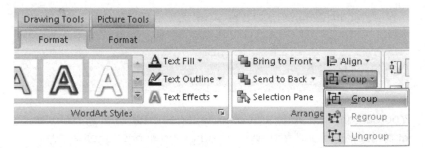

Figure 10.3
The Group command

2 Go to the **Drawing Tools Format** tab.

3 Click **Group** in the Arrange group.

4 Click **Regroup**, as shown in Figure 10.5.

Converting a SmartArt Graphic to Individual Shapes

SmartArt graphics are really just sophisticated layered objects. If you want to play with the various shapes within a SmartArt graphic, it's easy to do. When you make the conversions, each individual shape within the SmartArt graphic becomes a grouped shape that holds a geometric shape and a text box.

Important

Careful! Once a SmartArt graphic has been converted into individual objects, you can't convert it back. Also, all design and formatting tools from the SmartArt Tools tabs will be unavailable, although you can still format the new, individual objects using the Drawing Tools tab instead.

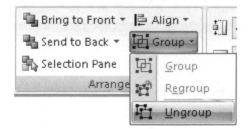

Figure 10.4
The Ungroup command

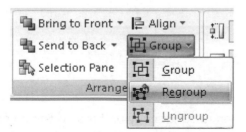

Figure 10.5
The Regroup command

To convert a SmartArt graphic into individual objects, follow these steps:

1 Select all shapes within the SmartArt graphic.

2 Go to the **Home** tab.

3 Click **Copy** in the Clipboard group, as shown in Figure 10.6.

4 Click a different area on the slide.

5 Go to the **Home** tab.

6 Click **Paste** in the Clipboard group.

Figure 10.6
The Copy command

Timesaver tip

To quickly select all shapes within a SmartArt graphic, click a shape within it, and then press **CTRL** + **A**.

→ Cutting, Copying and Pasting Objects

It's very common to cut or copy and then paste an object when working in PowerPoint. The most basic method for accomplishing this task involves these steps:

1 Right-click the object to be cut or copied.

2 In the shortcut menu, click **Cut** or **Copy**, as in Figure 10.7.

3 In the same or a different slide, right-click the location where you want the object pasted.

4 Click **Paste** in the shortcut menu.

> **Important**
>
> The Cut command will remove an item from your slide. If you do not immediately move it to another location using the Paste command, it will be deleted permanently as soon as you perform another command in PowerPoint.

There are some additional tricks to know about when copying and then pasting objects. The first is the Paste Special command; the second is the Office Clipboard.

Using the Paste Special Command

The Paste Special command is used when you need to copy and paste complex objects, such as Excel data and mathematical operations. If you copy or cut an item and then discover that it

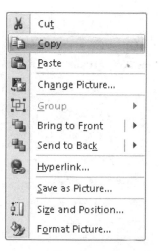

Figure 10.7
The Shortcut menu

will not paste using traditional paste methods, try the Paste Special command. Here's how to use it:

1. Cut or copy the object.

2. Click the new location for the object.

3. Go to the **Home** tab.

4. Click the arrow under Paste in the Clipboard group.

5. Click **Paste Special**, as in Figure 10.8.

Timesaver tip

Need to paste a hyperlink? Click the arrow under the Paste button of the Home tab's Clipboard group. Click **Paste as Hyperlink**.

Using the Office Clipboard

With Office 2007, you can use the Microsoft Office Clipboard to copy multiple objects from one program to another. The Clipboard allows you to copy items to it and then paste them into different Office documents as needed.

Figure 10.8
The Paste Special command

The Office Clipboard works with the commonly used Copy and Paste commands. It also works in conjunction with the Windows System Clipboard, which is a completely separate clipboard generated by your Windows operating system. The two clipboards can be a bit confusing; try to remember that the Paste command, the Paste button in PowerPoint and the keyboard shortcut **CTRL + V** will all paste the contents of the System Clipboard rather than the Office Clipboard. If you discover that an item is not pasting the way you thought it would, it's probably because you are not using the Paste options from the Office Clipboard.

To open the Office Clipboard, follow these steps:

1 Go to the **Home** tab.

2 Click the **Dialog Box Launcher** ⬚ in the Clipboard group.

The Office Clipboard will appear on your screen as a new task pane, as shown in Figure 10.9.

To control the display options for the Clipboard, follow these steps:

1 In the Clipboard task pane, click **Options**. It's located at the bottom of the task pane.

2 Click the display option you prefer, as Figure 10.10 shows.

You can close the Office Clipboard by clicking the **Close** button. ⨯

When you are ready to paste items from the Office Clipboard into the presentation, follow these steps:

1 On the slide, click the location where the pasted item will be located.

2 In the Clipboard task pane, double-click the item you want to paste.

Timesaver tip

You can paste multiple items by clicking the **Paste All** button in the Office Clipboard.

10

Figure 10.9
The Office Clipboard Task pane

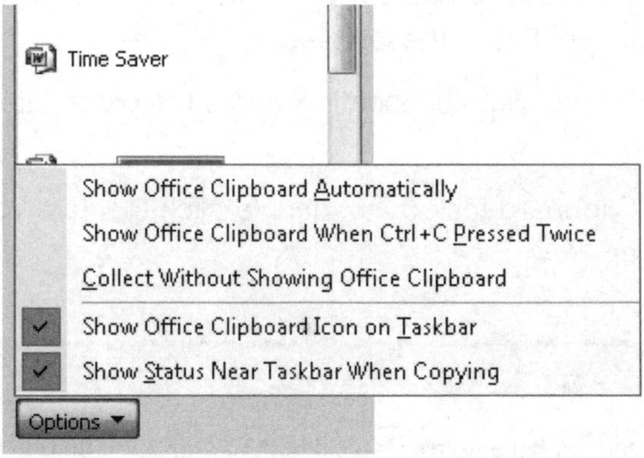

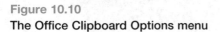

Figure 10.10
The Office Clipboard Options menu

→ Moving, Rotating and Resizing Objects

You'll discover that you often need to move objects within a PowerPoint slide. When objects are added to your slide, they are automatically stacked in layers. When objects overlap, as shown in Figure 10.11, it's easy to see how one stacks upon another.

> **Important**
>
> If you move a text pane associated with a SmartArt object, the change is only temporary. The next time you open PowerPoint, the Text pane will appear again in the default position.

Moving an Object

You can move any object very quickly by following these steps:

1 Click the object.

2 Hover the cursor over the border until it becomes a four-headed arrow.

3 Click and drag the object to its new location on the slide, as in Figure 10.12.

The Office

Figure 10.11
An example of stacked objects.

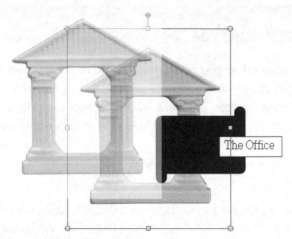

Figure 10.12
Object being dragged to new location

If you just want to move the object a tiny bit, hold **CTRL** on your keyboard and then press one of the keyboard arrow keys in the direction you need.

Timesaver tip

Need to move an object horizontally or vertically? Press and hold the **Shift** key on your keyboard while you drag the object.

Rotating an Object

Rotating objects is a fast and easy process in PowerPoint 2007. Follow these steps:

1 Click the object you want to rotate.

2 Grab the green handle with your cursor, as in Figure 10.13.

3 Pull the object in the direction you want it to rotate.

Need a more exact rotation? Take these steps:

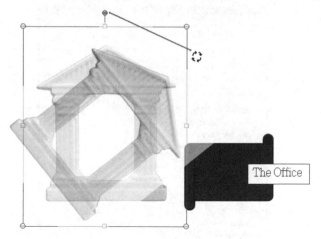

Figure 10.13
The Rotate handle

1 Click the object.

2 Go to the **Drawing Tools Format** tab. Note: if the object is a picture, go to the **Picture Tools Format** tab.

3 Click **Rotate** in the Arrange group.

4 Click **More Rotation Options**.

5 Enter the rotation specifications in the Rotation box under Size and Rotate, as shown in Figure 10.14.

Resizing an Object

Most of the time, you can resize an object in PowerPoint 2007 by clicking the border of the object and then dragging the border to the size you want once the cursor turns to a double arrow.

The cursor will turn to a double arrow when you hold it over one of the sizing handles on the object. These are tiny squares or circles on the border of the object, as shown in Figure 10.15. You can use these to resize an object vertically, horizontally or diagonally.

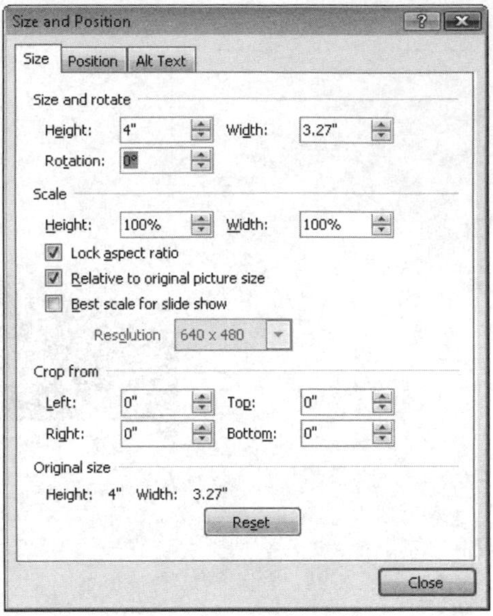

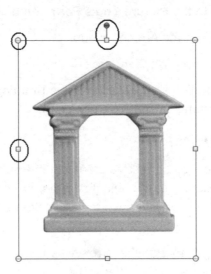

Figure 10.14
The Rotation dialogue box

Figure 10.15
Resizing handles

Resizing an Object to Exact Proportions

There might be times when you don't want an object to retain its original proportions. Instead, you might prefer to resize it to an exact proportion. In those cases, follow these steps for shapes, text boxes and WordArt:

1 Click the object.

2 Click the **Drawing Tools Format** tab.

3 Click the **Dialog Box Launcher** ▣ in the Size group.

4 In the Size tab, change to the Scale percentages you want, using the arrows in the Height and/or Width boxes.

5 Make sure there is not a checkmark in the Lock Aspect Ratio box, as shown in Figure 10.16.

6 Click **Close**.

The same steps apply to pictures, with the exception of step 2. Instead, click the **Picture Tools Format** tab.

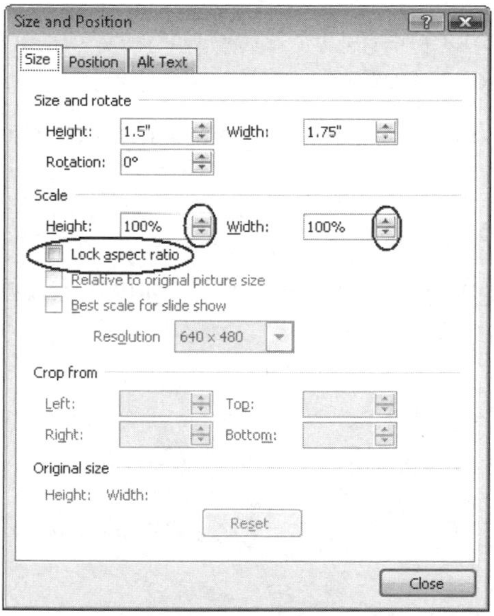

Figure 10.16
The Size and Position dialogue box

Resizing a Table

When you resize a table, you can maintain the height and width ratio by pressing and holding the **Shift** key on your keyboard as you drag the borders for resizing. Or, you can enter a specific table size by following these steps:

1 Click the table.

2 Go to the **Table Tools Layout** tab.

3 Enter the new table specifications in the Height and Width boxes in the Table Size group.

Resizing a Column or Row

Need to resize all columns or rows in a table? Follow these steps:

1 Click the table.

2 Go to the **Table Tools Layout** tab.

3 Enter your column or row specifications in the Height and/or Width boxes in the Cell Size group, as Figure 10.17 shows.

Note: the minimum height for a row will vary, depending upon the font size you are using.

If you just need to change one or a few rows or columns, follow these steps:

1 Click the table.

2 Hover the cursor over the row or column border that needs resizing.

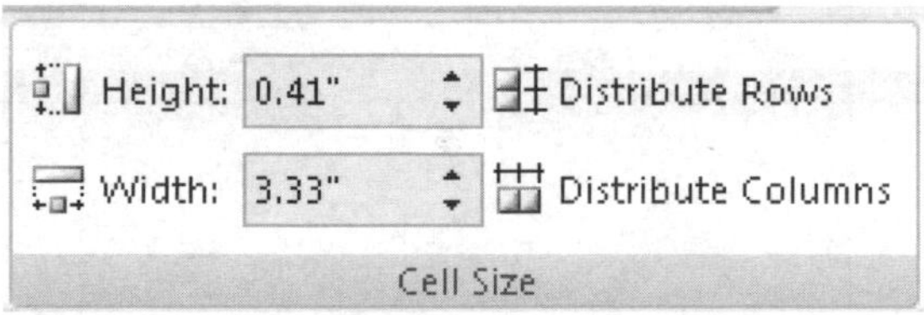

Figure 10.17
Column and Row specifications

3 When the cursor changes to a double arrow with double lines, click and drag the cell border to the height or width desired, as in Figure 10.18.

Resizing a SmartArt Object

You can resize individual objects in a SmartArt graphic, or the entire graphic, in the same way you would resize any other object. However, in some SmartArt graphics, the remaining shapes might adjust their size or position as well. The individual text within the shapes will resize automatically to fit the new shape unless you have specifically customised the text. Another quick way to resize an individual shape within a SmartArt graphic is to follow these steps:

1 Click the individual shape.

2 Go to the **SmartArt Tools Format** tab.

3 Click **Larger** or **Smaller** in the Shapes group, as shown in Figure 10.19.

You can adjust multiple shapes in a SmartArt graphic using these steps as well – just press and hold down **CTRL** on your keyboard after step 1, and then select additional shapes.

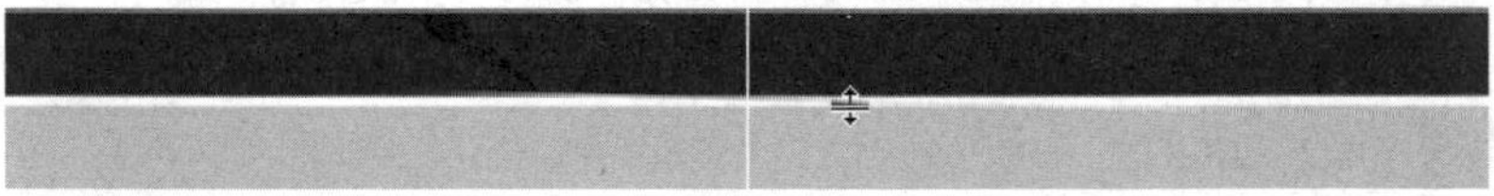

Figure 10.18
Dragging a cell border

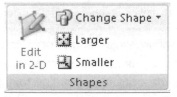

Figure 10.19
SmartArt resizing options

Resizing Headers and Footers

When you use a header or a footer in your presentation, you might discover that it needs to be resized. To do that, follow these steps:

1 Go to the **View** tab.

2 Click the **Slide Master** tab.

3 Click the Slide Master that holds the header or footer you want to change.

4 Click the header or footer placeholder.

5 Use a sizing handle to resize the object to your specifications.

Working with Grids and Guidelines

To make aligning objects on a slide easier, you have the option of working with grids and guidelines – dotted lines that cover the slide so that you can easily line up different items horizontally and vertically.

By default, grids and guidelines are not shown. To show them as you work on a slide, follow these steps:

1 Right-click the slide.

2 Click **Grids and Guidelines**.

3 Place a checkmark next to Display Grid on Screen, as shown in Figure 10.20.

4 Click **OK**.

> **Important**
>
> Don't worry if you forget to turn off grids and guidelines. They won't show when your presentation is run in Slide Show format.

The Snap to Grid option, which aligns objects to the nearest grid intersection on the slide, is switched on automatically in PowerPoint 2007 in order to help you line things up quickly. You can temporarily remove this option by pressing and holding the **ALT** key on your keyboard while you drag an object.

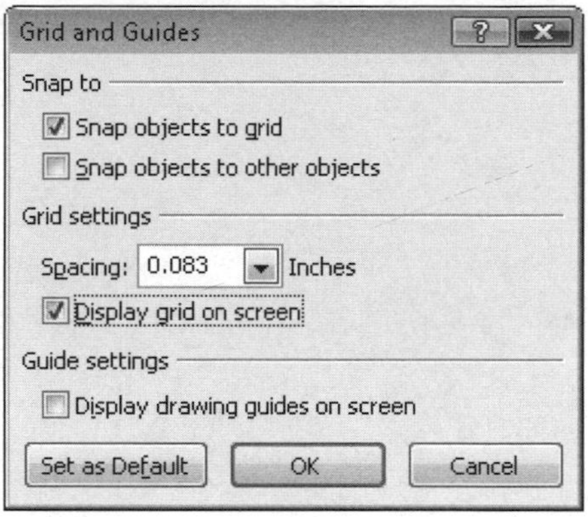

Figure 10.20
The Grids and Guidelines dialogue box

To turn off this option permanently, however, follow these steps:

1 Right-click the slide you are working with.

2 Click **Grids and Guides**.

3 Clear the checkmark from Snap Objects to Grid.

4 Click **OK**.

If you prefer to make this new setting your default, click **Set as Default** instead of clicking **OK** in step 4, as Figure 10.21 shows.

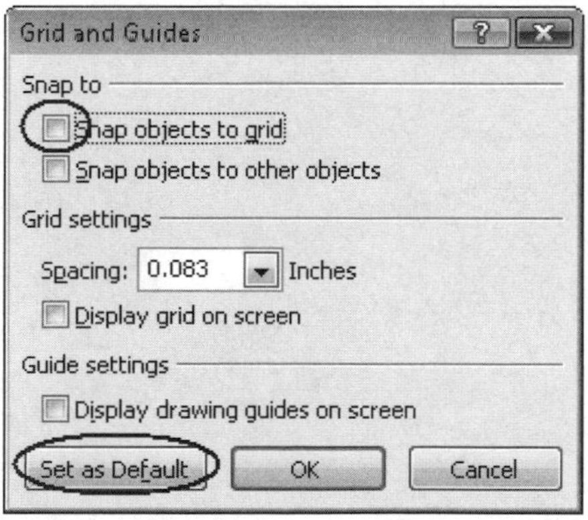

Figure 10.21
The Set as Default command

11

Working with Slide Shows

In this chapter, you will learn how to rehearse your slide show and how to work with slide timings, record narration, use the Presenter View and write on slides during a presentation. You'll also discover how to create custom shows and photo albums.

You should always rehearse your slide show to see how it displays. This preview process will help you verify that there aren't any errors – such as text that drops off a slide. It will also help you review timings, transitions and special effects to be certain they are all working as expected.

To start a slide show, follow these steps:

1 Open your presentation.

2 Go to the **Slide Show** tab.

3 Click **From Beginning** in the Start Slide Show group, as shown in Figure 11.1.

Figure 11.1
Slide Show Rehearsal options

You can also start your show from the current slide you have selected by clicking **From Current Slide**.

The slide show will play as you set it up, so either click the mouse as needed to move slides along or watch as the slides play automatically.

Rehearsing the Timing of Your Presentation

Next, take some time to rehearse the delivery of your presentation as the slide show plays. This will help you check the timing is correct and let you see how the slides flow as you speak.

To rehearse your slide show, follow these steps:

1 Open your presentation, and go to the **Slide Show** tab.

2 Click **Rehearse Timings** in the Set Up group, as Figure 11.2 shows. A Rehearsal toolbar will appear on your screen as the slide show plays to show you the timing of your presentation (see Figure 11.3). You can also use the toolbar to advance to the next slide, pause and repeat the slide as necessary. It also shows the timing for each slide and for the overall presentation.

3 After you set the timing on the last slide, a message box will appear with the total time for the presentation. If you want to keep the recorded slide timings, click **Yes**; if you do not, click **No**.

4 If you keep the slide timings, Slide Sorter view will appear and show you the presentation and the time.

The next time you play the slide show, the rehearsed timings will automatically advance the slides for you. This kind of automatic timing is great for many presentations, but you might not always want to use slide timing. For example, some audiences might require a lengthier explanation on certain slides; a preset timing

11

Figure 11.2
Rehearsal Timings options

Figure 11.3
The Rehearsal toolbar

for that slide, then, can advance your slide before you are ready. However, you might not want to delete the timings permanently.

If you want to remove rehearsed slide timing temporarily, follow these steps:

1 Go to the **Slide Show** tab.

2 Clear the Use Rehearsed Timings checkbox in the Set Up group.

To begin using rehearsed timings again, simply go back and select the Use Rehearsed Timings checkbox.

Setting Slide Timings Manually

If you prefer to set the timing for your slides manually instead of using the timings provided when rehearsing your presentation, follow these steps:

1 Click the slide you want to set the timing for.

2 Go to the **Animations** tab.

3 In the Advance Slide section of the Transition to This Slide group, place a checkmark to the left of the Automatically After box, shown in Figure 11.4.

4 In the Timing box, enter the number of seconds you want the slide to play.

Important

To record narration, you need a microphone for your computer.

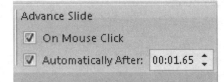

Figure 11.4
Advance Slide options

Adding Narration

Adding narration to a presentation is a useful option in many ways. You can record a narration before you run the presentation, or you can record as the presentation runs so that you can capture audience comments. You can also record comments on selected slides.

> ## Important
>
> Voice narration takes precedence over other automatic sounds you might have included in a presentation. This means that sounds set to play automatically will be overridden by a narration. However, sounds set to play on click will still play when you click them.

When you record a narration, PowerPoint will record the amount of time you take for each slide. You will be prompted to save these timings, but you don't have to accept them. However, accepting them is useful if you want the presentation to run automatically with the narration.

Narrations can be either embedded in or linked to the presentation. Both options offer benefits. Embedded narration means the sound file becomes part of the presentation itself and will move with the presentation from computer to computer. Linked narration lets you have a smaller file, but links must be moved every time you move the presentation. However, in a linked narration, you can go back later and edit sound files separately from the presentation using a sound editing program.

To record a narration before using a presentation, follow these steps:

1 In Normal view, click the slide where the narration will begin.

2 Go to the **Slide Show** tab.

3 Click **Record Narration** in the Set Up group, as shown in Figure 11.5.

4 Click **Set Microphone Level** and follow the directions.

Figure 11.5
The Record Narration command

5 When finished with the microphone directions, click **OK**.

6 To embed the narration, click **OK** and go to step 8. To link the narration, go to step 7.

7 To link to the narration, place a checkmark in the Link Narrations In box and click **Browse**. Select the location to save the narration and click **Select**. It's a good idea, but not essential, to place your narrations in the same folder as the presentation.

8 Speak into the microphone, clicking slides to advance from one to the next.

9 Click the black Exit screen. You will be prompted to save the timings for the presentation. Click **Save** if you want to keep them; click **Don't Save** if you don't want to.

To preview the narration, follow these steps:

1 Click the sound icon on the first slide where the narration occurs.

2 Go to the **Sound Tools Options** tab.

3 Click **Preview** in the Play group.

→ Using Presenter View

A terrific new feature in PowerPoint 2007 is the Presenter View, which gives you the ability to use two monitors as you present a slide show. This feature lets you run other programs that your audience never sees; it's extremely helpful if you need to refer to your speaker notes in the file, for example, or need to check what the next click or slide will bring.

To use the Presenter View, you must have a computer that has a multiple-monitor capability turned on or a laptop with a dual display feature. With this feature, you can do the following:

■ Use thumbnails to select slides out of sequence.

■ Preview text so that you know exactly what will happen on the next click.

■ See speaker notes in a large font size.

■ Black out screen content as needed and resume where you left off.

To turn on multiple-monitor support in PowerPoint 2007, follow these steps:

1 Open the presentation.

2 Go to the **Slide Show** tab.

3 Go to the **Monitors** group.

4 Place a checkmark in the Use Presenter View checkbox, as Figure 11.6 shows.

5 Click the arrow next to Show Presentation On, and then click the name of the monitor you want to use, as in Figure 11.7.

After you have set up the monitors properly, you can deliver the presentation using Presenter View. Follow these steps:

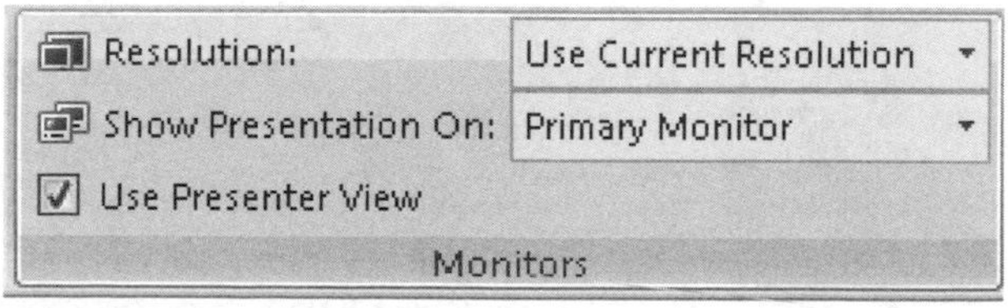

Figure 11.6
Use Presenter View command

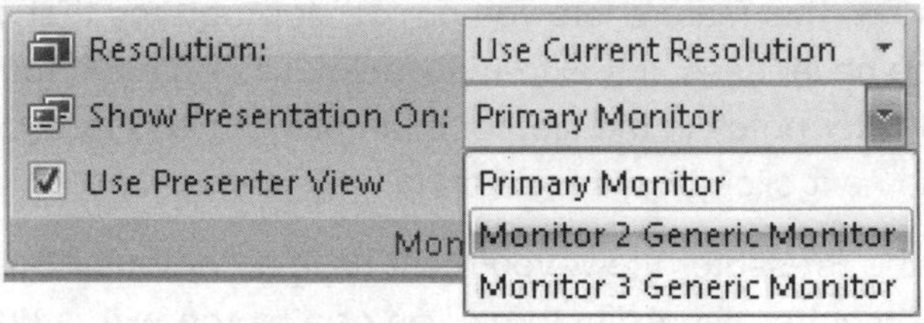

Resolution:	Use Current Resolution ▾
Show Presentation On:	Primary Monitor ▾
☑ Use Presenter View	Primary Monitor
Mon	**Monitor 2 Generic Monitor**
	Monitor 3 Generic Monitor

Figure 11.7
You must select the monitor for the Presenter View

1 Open the presentation.

2 Go to the **Slide Show** tab.

3 Click **Set Up Slide Show** in the Set Up group, as shown in
Figure 11.8.

4 In the Set Up Show dialogue box, choose the options you
want:

■ If you have narration or animations that you prefer not to
use during the presentation, clear the corresponding
checkboxes under Show options.

■ Change pen colours in Show options if you decide to
write on slides during your presentation.

■ Verify that the correct monitor is selected under Multiple
monitors and that the Show Presenter View checkbox is
selected, as in Figure 11.9.

5 Click **OK**.

6 When you are ready to begin delivery, go to the **View** tab,
and click **Slide Show** in the Presentation Views group.

Figure 11.8
The Set Up Slide Show command

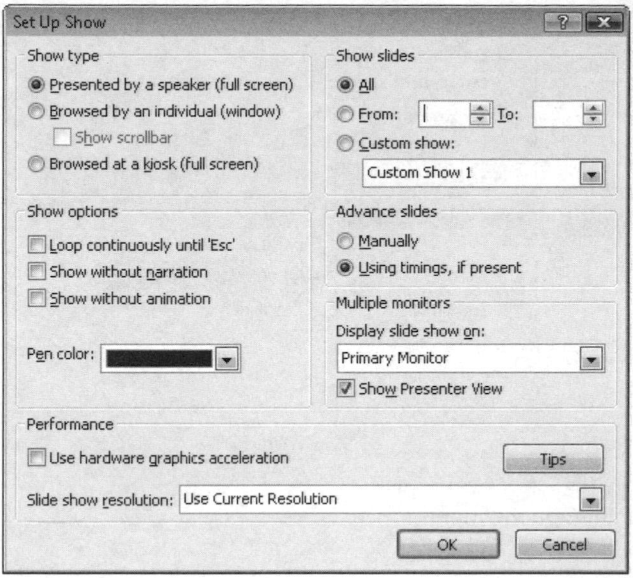

Figure 11.9
The Set Up Show dialogue box

→ Writing on Slides During a Presentation

As you give a presentation, you can add text to it by using the pen or highlighter option. To circle, underline, draw arrows or make similar marks in order to grab audience attention during a presentation, you must be in the Slide Show view. Then follow these steps:

1 Right-click the slide you want to write on.

2 Click **Pointer Options**. In the shortcut menu, choose **Ballpoint Pen**, **Felt Tip Pen** or **Highlighter**, as shown in Figure 11.10. Change the colour of the pointer by selecting **Ink Color** and choosing a new colour.

3 Hold down the left mouse button and drag the cursor to draw or write as needed.

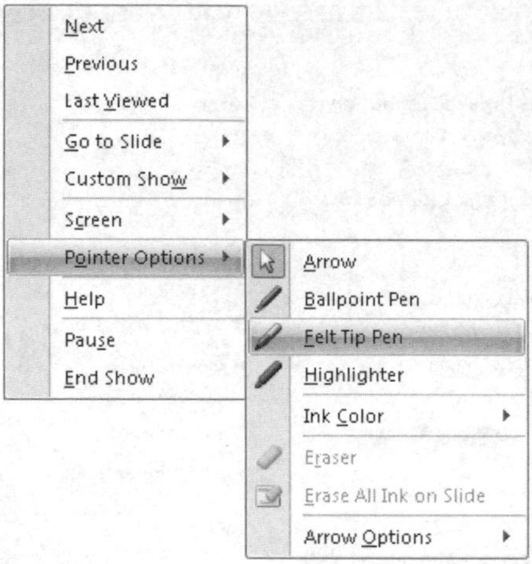

Figure 11.10
The Pointer Options menu

To erase all marks on a slide, choose **Erase All Ink on Slide**. This will erase all marks, regardless of when they were made. To erase individual marks on the slide, follow these steps:

1 Right-click the slide.

2 Click **Eraser** under Pointer Options.

3 Click on the mark you want to erase. Note: this will erase all marks made by the pen before the pen was last lifted. If you don't lift your pen occasionally, you will erase all marks on the slide with one click of the eraser.

→ Creating Custom Shows

A custom show allows you to take one show – a single presentation – and adapt it quickly and easily for a variety of audiences. If you have ever cut and pasted slides from one presentation in order to create a new, almost identical presentation for a new audience, you will love this feature.

Custom shows are created in one of two ways: basic or hyperlinked. A basic custom show is a separate presentation that includes some slides from your original presentation. A hyperlinked custom show lets you create additional custom shows that link to the primary presentation.

Creating a Basic Custom Show

Here's how a basic custom show works: if your presentation has a total of 20 slides, then you can create a custom show named Show 1 that includes just slides 4, 6, 8 and 12. A second custom show – Show 2 – could contain slides 2, 3, 6 and 17.

With this method, you can use one presentation while choosing specific slides within that presentation to meet your audience's needs. It's a single presentation with the same information for everyone, but you can choose which information to display to different audiences.

11

Important

If you create a basic custom show from a presentation, you can always run the entire presentation in its original sequence.

Here are the steps to create a basic custom show:

1. Open the presentation.

2. Go to the **Slide Show** tab.

3. Click **Custom Slide Show** in the Start Slide Show group.

4. Click **Custom Shows**, as in Figure 11.11.

5. In the Custom Shows dialogue box, click **New**.

6. In the Define Custom Show dialogue box, select the slides you want to show your first audience under Slides In Presentation. Just use the **Add** and **Remove** buttons as needed to add more slides and remove slides, as Figure 11.12 shows. Also, the up and down arrows will allow you to move slides into a new sequence.

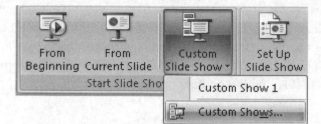

Figure 11.11
The Custom Show menu

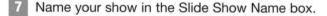

Figure 11.12
The Define Custom Show dialogue box

7 Name your show in the Slide Show Name box.

8 Click **OK**. The Custom Shows dialogue box will reappear. Click **New** again if you need to make another show, and click **Edit**, **Remove** or **Copy** to make those changes instead.

9 When you have completed making custom shows and edits as needed, click **Close** in the Custom Shows dialogue box.

To see how the custom show will appear to audiences, follow these steps:

1 Go to the **Slide Show** tab.

2 Click **Custom Slide Show** in the Start Slide Show group.

3 Select a show to preview.

4 Click **Show**.

Timesaver tip

To select multiple sequential slides, click the first slide, and then hold down the **Shift** key on the keyboard while you click the last slide that you want to select. To select multiple but non-sequential slides, hold down **Ctrl** while you click each slide that you want to select.

Creating a Hyperlinked Custom Show

If you want to create a primary presentation and then customise that presentation for a variety of different audiences, you can create a primary custom show that uses hyperlinks to let you move easily between audience presentations.

11

With this method, you will create completely different slides for each audience using one presentation, but each audience sees only the slides applicable to it. The advantage here is that you can have essentially one presentation with slides applicable to all audiences as well as mini customised presentations within it.

Follow these steps to create a hyperlinked custom show:

1 Open the presentation.

2 Go to the **Slide Show** tab.

3 Click **Custom Slide Show** in the Start Slide Show group.

4 Click **Custom Shows**.

5 In the Custom Shows dialogue box, click **New**.

6 In the Define Custom Show dialogue box, select the slides you want to show your first audience under Slides In Presentation. Use the **Add** and **Remove** buttons as needed to add more slides or remove slides as you build your custom slide show. Use the up and down arrows to move slides into a new sequence.

7 Name your show in the Slide Show Name box.

8 Click **OK**. The Custom Shows dialogue box will reappear. Click **New** again if you need to make another show, and click **Edit**, **Remove** or **Copy** to make those changes instead.

9 When you have completed making custom shows and edits as needed, click **Close**.

10 Select the text or object you want to use as your hyperlink. Go to the **Links** group on the Insert tab, and click **Hyperlink**.

11 In the Insert Hyperlink dialogue box, select **Place In This Document** under Link To.

12 Under Select A Place In This Document, select the custom show you want to link to, and then select the Show And Return checkbox. Click **OK**.

Running a Custom Show

Now that you've created a custom show, you're going to want to show it to someone. Opening a custom show is a slightly different process from opening a standard presentation. Just follow these steps:

1 Open the presentation, and go to the **Slide Show** tab.

2 Click **Custom Slide Show** in the Start Slide Show group.

3 Select the custom show from the list provided. The show will begin automatically.

Timesaver tip

Hyperlinked custom shows let you create a table-of-contents slide so you can navigate to different sections of your presentation quickly.

→ Using Photo Albums

A fun, easy way to share a collection of images is through the use of photo albums in PowerPoint. All you need are digital images on your hard disk drive or CD; then you add them to PowerPoint with the effects you want.

To create a photo album, follow these steps:

1 Open a new presentation.

2 Go to the **Insert** tab.

3 Click the arrow under Photo Album in the Illustrations group.

4 Click **New Photo Album**, as shown in Figure 11.13.

5 In the Photo Album dialogue box, click **File/Disk** under Insert Picture From, as Figure 11.14 shows.

11

6 In the Insert New Pictures dialogue box, select the picture you want, and then click **Insert**.

7 Continue selecting photos until finished.

8 Under Album Layout in the Photo Album dialogue box, select the picture layout for each page in your album, and choose a shape for the frame, as in Figure 11.15. If you want to, apply a theme in this section as well.

9 Under Picture Options, select the appropriate checkbox to place captions below all pictures or to change all pictures to

Figure 11.13
The Photo Album command

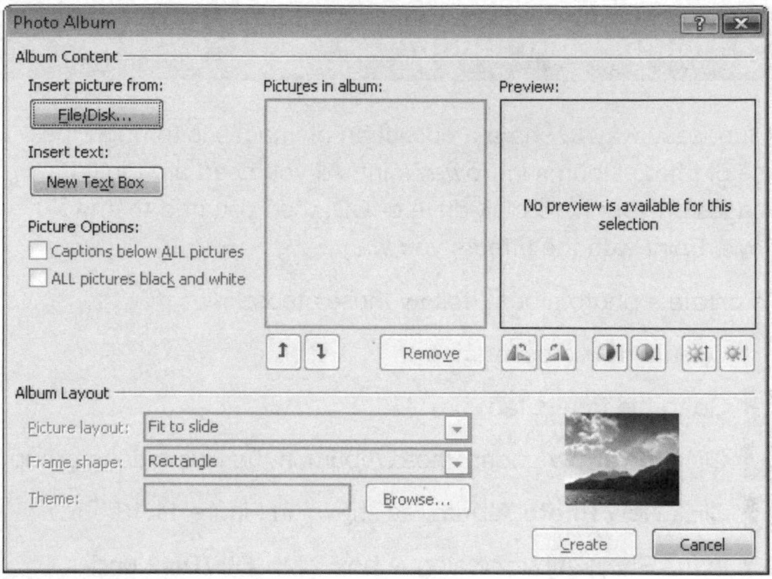

Figure 11.14
The Photo Album dialogue box

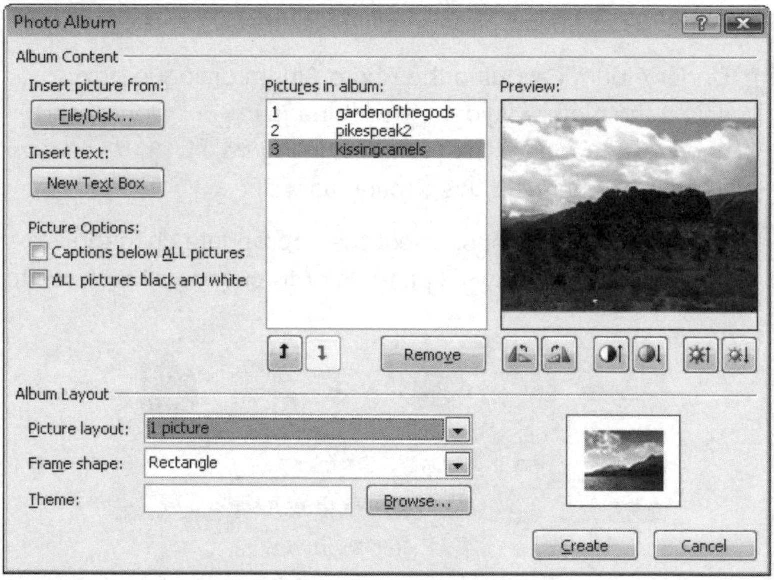

Figure 11.15
Picture Layout options

black and white. Note: you cannot selectively add captions or black-and-white colouring here.

10 Use the arrows to change the placement of your pictures.

11 Use the **Rotate**, **Contrast** and **Brightness** buttons to rotate individual pictures or change their brightness or contrast.

12 Click **Create**.

You can change the pictures in your photo album very quicly. Just follow these steps:

1 Open the photo album presentation.

2 Go to the **Insert** tab.

3 Click the arrow under Photo Album in the Illustrations group.

4 Click **Edit Photo Album**, as shown in Figure 11.16.

5 In the Edit Photo Album dialogue box, make changes as desired (you can also add or remove photos here).

6 Click **Update**.

Working with Captions in Your Photo Album

You can add a caption to your pictures with the Edit Photo Album dialogue box, under the Picture Options section. Watch for the following:

■ If the Captions below ALL pictures checkbox isn't available, you need to specify a layout for the pictures in your photo album.

Figure 11.16
The Edit Photo Album command

- Be sure Fit To Slide is not the layout you select – this option leaves no room for captions.

If you want to move the caption to another location on the slide, just select the caption box and drag it to the location you prefer. To change the caption font, select the caption text and make changes using the commands in the Font group on the Home tab.

Publishing Your Photo Album to the Web

One easy way to share your album with friends and family is to publish it to the Web rather than struggle with e-mail inbox size limits and spam blockers. To publish a photo album to the Web, follow these steps:

1. Open the photo album you want to publish to the Web.

2. Click the **Microsoft Office** button.

3. Click **Save As**.

4. Click **PowerPoint 97–2003 Presentation**.

5. Select the path or location for the Web page on a Web server in the Address bar.

6. Type a file name in the File Name box, or accept the suggested name.

7. In the Save As Type list, click **Web Page**.

8. Click **Change Title**, and type the title bar text in the Page Title box if you want something different displayed in browser title bars.

9. Click **OK**.

10. Click **Publish**. When the Publish As Web Page dialogue box opens, set the following options:

   - Decide whether to publish the complete presentation or just certain slides.

   - Choose the desired browser support.

- Verify the file name for accuracy.

- Select the **Open Published Web Page In Browser** checkbox.

11 Click **Publish**.

Note: when you see the photo album displayed in the browser, take note of the URL. It might not always be what you expected!

11

12

Completing Your Presentation

In this chapter, you will learn how to decide what to print and how to work with the Quick Print Option, change page setups and use Print Preview. You'll also discover how to publish your presentation to a slide library.

→ Choosing what to Print

There are many different ways to print a presentation once it's ready for distribution. You can print handouts and notes pages, and even print in Outline view. Before you print, consider your audience. Will it help them to have multiple slides on a printed page along with space to take notes? Maybe they would benefit from a larger view of the slides instead.

You can print your presentation in different paper sizes, too, and set colour options and margins to meet your needs. You can print in the following colour and black-and-white formats:

- **Color** – this option prints in colour when you use a colour printer.

- **Color (On Black and White Printer)** – this option prints in greyscale if you use a black-and-white printer.

- **Grayscale** – this option prints variations of grey tones between black and white. Background fills are printed as white, so that the text will be more legible. (Note: greyscale can sometimes appear the same as pure black and white.)

- **Pure Black and White** – this option prints the handout with no grey fills.

Timesaver tip

PowerPoint will set the colours in your presentation to match your printer's capabilities.

→ Using Print Preview

Once you have decided which print option you need, use Print Preview to help you spot graphics and text boxes that might be falling off a page, for example, and to show you other potential print problems.

To use Print Preview, follow these steps:

1 Open the presentation.

2 Click the **Microsoft Office** button.

3 Go to **Print** and click **Print Preview**, as in Figure 12.1.

In the Print Preview screen, you will see a completely new tab called Print Preview. This tab has several groups: Print, Page Setup, Zoom and Preview, as Figure 12.2 shows.

■ To change the headers and footers or the colour setup, click **Options** in the Print group.

■ To change the print options (slides, handouts, notes pages or outline), make your selections in the Page Setup group under Print What. Note: if you select **Handouts**, you also need to tell

12

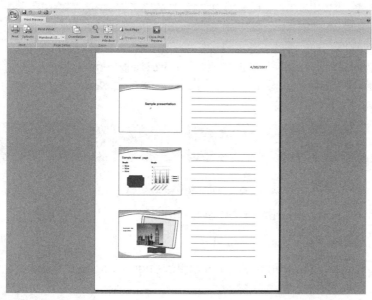

Figure 12.1
This sample Print Preview shows a presentation to be printed in handouts.

Figure 12.2
The Print Preview tab

PowerPoint how many slides per page are desired and whether you want them placed horizontally or vertically.

■ Apply the **Zoom**, **Fit to Window** and **Next Page/Previous Page** commands as needed.

When you are satisfied that the printing output will appear as desired, click **Close Print Preview** in the Preview group to return to the presentation and move to the Print dialogue box.

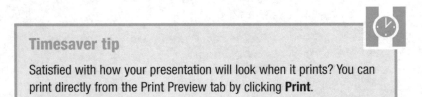

Timesaver tip

Satisfied with how your presentation will look when it prints? You can print directly from the Print Preview tab by clicking **Print**.

→ Printing Your Presentation

To print your presentation, follow these steps:

1 Click the **Microsoft Office** button.

2 Go to **Print** and click **Print**.

3 In the Print Range section of the Print dialogue box, select the slides you want printed.

4 Specify the number of copies to print under Copies, as Figure 12.3 shows.

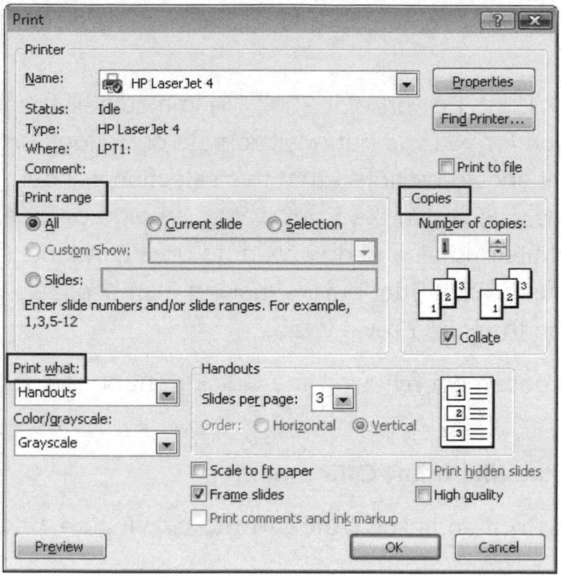

Figure 12.3
The Print dialogue box

5 If you did not select a print option during Print Preview,
select one now (**Notes, Handouts, Outline** or **Slides**).

6 Make any other desired selections.

7 Click **OK**.

Timesaver tip

Go to **Print Preview** from the Print dialogue box instead of going
through the **Microsoft Office** button. Just click the **Preview** button in
the bottom left corner of the dialogue box.

→ Using the Quick Print Option

You may have noticed another printing choice called Quick Print.
If you have already gone through your presentation and are

confident that it needs no further changes, you can use this command.

With Quick Print, PowerPoint 2007 will immediately print the presentation for you without any prompts or options for changes. However, it should be noted that this selection will default to the last options selected in the Print dialogue box. So, for example, if you last printed notes and now want to print handouts, you shouldn't use Quick Print before making the necessary printing changes on the Print Preview tab.

To print a document by using the Quick Print option, follow these steps:

1 Click the **Microsoft Office** button.

2 Go to **Print** and click **Quick Print**, as in Figure 12.4.

Figure 12.4
The Quick Print command

→ Changing Page Setup

For changes to your slide page setup, you'll need to access the Page Setup dialogue box. To open it, follow these steps:

1 Go to the **Design** tab.

2 Click **Page Setup** in the Page Setup group, as shown in Figure 12.5.

This dialogue box lets you make changes to slide orientation for the screen. It offers some other features, too. You can do the following:

- Manually change the slide width and height.

- Select predetermined options for slide sizing so you can easily set up your slides for different screen and paper sizes, as well as for overheads, banners and custom sizes.

- Orient the print to accommodate notes, handouts and outlines.

12

Timesaver tip

Need a higher-quality print job? Select **High Quality** in the Print dialogue box. You can change the resolution, blend transparent graphics and print soft shadows when this option is selected.

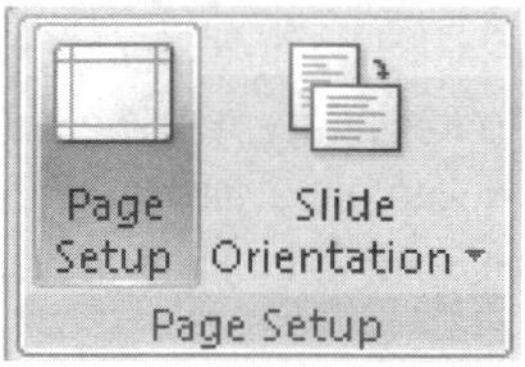

Figure 12.5
The Page Setup command

→ Publishing Your Presentation to a Slide Library

PowerPoint 2007 works in conjunction with SharePoint Server 2007, which allows people to connect to documents, calendars, contacts and tasks across a network. If your organisation uses SharePoint Server 2007, you can take advantage of PowerPoint slide libraries.

These libraries let you store slides in a central, shared location so that everyone on the network can share and reuse the information. Every time an existing slide is changed in the library, a time stamp is placed on it and the file is checked out to the user. The library also has features to help you locate the latest version of a slide and to track and review changes to slides.

Slide libraries let you merge presentations easily and quickly through the use of linked presentations. When copies of a slide or presentation are linked within a slide library, changes to the original presentation are synchronised in designated copies. Changes in copies of the original presentation will also synchronise with the original presentation. Plus, when you open a linked presentation, PowerPoint 2007 will ask whether you want to check for slide updates.

Important

A slide library must be established on a SharePoint Server before any slides can be published to the library. A network administrator typically sets that up. The option will not be available to you in the Microsoft Office button if you are not on a SharePoint Server.

Publishing Slides to a Slide Library

Presentations must be saved to your hard drive before they can be published to a slide library. Then, follow these steps to publish slides to a slide library:

1 Click the **Microsoft Office** button.

2 Go to **Publish** and click **Publish Slides**.

3 In the Publish Slides dialogue box, select all the slides to be published to the library. Note: you can select all the slides by pressing the **Select All** button.

4 Enter a name in the File Name box.

5 Type a description into the Description box.

6 Enter or select the location of the slide library in the Publish To list.

7 Click **Publish**.

12

Important

PowerPoint automatically names and assigns a unique identifier for each slide file. Moving slides after they have been published means your slides will no longer appear in sequential order, which could impact your retrieval of them at a later date.

To check for changes on slides from a slide library, follow these steps:

1 Open a presentation with slides from a slide library.

2 In the Check For Slide Updates dialogue box, click **Check**.

3 Click **OK** if the There Are No Updated Slides At This Time, Click OK message appears. Otherwise, go to step 4.

4 If the Confirm Slide Update dialogue box appears, compare the thumbnails to determine whether to replace your local slide with a new one from the library, or whether you want to add a new one from the library to your presentation so you can compare them at full size.

5 Click **Replace** to replace any slides.

6 Click **Append** to add a slide for further comparison. The new slide will appear after the old one in your presentation.

You can also add slides from the slide library directly into your presentation. To add a slide from a slide library, follow these steps:

1 Open the presentation to which the slide will be added.

2 Go to the **Home** tab.

3 Click the arrow under New Slide in the Slides group.

4 Click **Reuse Slides**.

5 In the Reuse Slides pane, type the location of the slide library in the Insert Slide From box.

6 To find the correct slide library, click the horizontal arrow or **Browse**.

7 In the All Slides list, click the slide you want to add to your presentation.

8 Repeat steps 4–7 until you have added all the slides you want.

Timesaver tip

You can ask to be notified when a slide used in your presentation is changed in the slide library. At the bottom of the Reuse Slides pane, click the slide, and then select the Tell Me When This Slide Changes checkbox.

brilliant
pocket books